Evaluating, Improving, and Judging Faculty Performance in Two-Year Colleges

Evaluating, Improving, and Judging Faculty Performance in Two-Year Colleges

Richard I. Miller
Charles Finley
Candace Shedd Vancko

BERGIN & GARVEY
Westport, Connecticut • London

Library of Congress Cataloging-in-Publication Data

Miller, Richard I.
    Evaluating, improving, and judging faculty performance in two-year colleges / by Richard I. Miller, Charles Finley, and Candace Shedd Vancko.
        p. cm.
    Includes bibliographical references (p.) and index.
    ISBN 0–89789–692–0 (alk. paper)
    1. Community college teachers—Rating of—United States.
    2. Community college teachers—In-service training—United States.
    I. Finley, Charles. II. Vancko, Candace Shedd. III. Title.
    LB2333.M49 2000
    378.1'224—dc21   99–22083

British Library Cataloguing in Publication Data is available.

Copyright © 2000 by Richard I. Miller, Charles Finley, and Candace Shedd Vancko

Library of Congress Catalog Card Number: 99–22083
ISBN: 0–89789–692–0

First published in 2000

Bergin & Garvey, 88 Post Road West, Westport, CT 06881
An imprint of Greenwood Publishing Group, Inc.
www.greenwood.com

Printed in the United States of America

The paper used in this book complies with the Permanent Paper Standard issued by the National Information Standards Organization (Z39.48–1984).

10 9 8 7 6 5 4 3 2 1

Contents

Exhibits   vii

Preface   ix

Introduction   xi

1   Assessing Your Institution's Climate for Evaluation and Development   1

2   Focus on Teaching   19

3   Improving Part-Time Teaching   33

4   Designing and Implementing Faculty Evaluation Systems   45

5   Focus on Improving   67

6   Designing and Implementing Professional Improvement Systems   81

7   Making Faculty Personnel Decisions   93

8   Moving into the Twenty-First Century   113

Epilogue   125

Appendix A   Recommended Improvements in Evaluation   129

Appendix B   Teaching/Learning Values at Miami-Dade
              Community College   131

Appendix C   Summary of Studies Used to Evaluate
              Teaching Performance   135

Appendix D   Classroom Visitation Evaluation   137

Appendix E   Self-Evaluation of Teaching   139

Appendix F   Teaching Materials Evaluation   141

Appendix G   Steps to Consider in Developing a Faculty
              Evaluation System   143

Appendix H   Principles of Learning   159

Appendix I   Annual Performance Review   163

References   171

Index   183

Exhibits

1.1 Evaluating Overall Faculty Performance   4

1.2 Planning-Doing (Leading-Managing)-Evaluating
     Model   9

2.1 Top Ten Ranking Characteristics of Effective
     Community College Teachers from 1920 to 1989   28

2.2 Evaluating Faculty Teaching Performance   29

4.1 Student Rating of Classroom Teaching   52

4.2 Faculty Service and Relations Evaluation   61

4.3 Student Evaluation of Instructor Advising   64

5.1 The Extent to Which 23 Development Practices Are
     Used in 50 Percent or More of 281 Community and
     Technical Colleges and Their Overall Ratings   73

6.1 A Conceptual Framework for Developing,
     Managing, and Evaluating a Faculty Development
     Program   84

6.2 Training and Development Matrix   87

6.3 Training and Development Matrix: New Faculty
     Member Wanting Pedagogical Skills   89

6.4 Training and Development Matrix: Chairperson
     Wanting Administrative Skills for Promotion
     to Dean   90

6.5 Professional Growth Evaluation   91

7.1 A Conceptual Framework for Individualizing
     Professional Responsibilities   108

7.2 Performance Profile—Instructor A   109

7.3 Performance Profile—Instructor B   110

Preface

The worlds of evaluating, improving, and judging faculty performances are paramount issues in American post-secondary education,
and no end is in sight. Always important issues—matters of instruction, curriculum, quality control, and quantity factors relating
to financing and prioritization—have given assessment (how much
and what) and evaluation (how good) their current status.

This book focuses upon the two-year college sector, which edu-
cates over 40 percent of the total post-secondary student population. The remarkable growth patterns of these colleges in the 1960s
and 1970s, when technical and community colleges were being
built at an astounding rate, have flattened out and these hundreds
of colleges are now vital parts of the U.S. post-secondary scene.
Attention now is turning to the issues of planning, leadership and
management, and formative and summative evaluation.

Initially the literature pertaining to research and teaching evaluation relied almost exclusively upon data from four-year colleges,
and much has been learned and applied from this borrowing.
However, increasingly more primary elements and processes that
are involved in the institutional dynamics of making these decisions in two-year colleges come from two-year college data.

We have sought to write a practical book—one that combines
research and practice—that also provides useful ideas and approaches whether they be conceptual frameworks, research theories and practices, or how-to-do-it approaches to improving
teaching and learning.

Introduction

This book provides a comprehensive picture of how faculty teaching evaluation can be improved, and also focuses on improving faculty teaching in two-year colleges. Much work remains to be done in this important area, but very meager research findings and practical guidance are available to provide assistance. With current slowdowns in hiring new faculty members and with an aging instructional staff, the challenges of developing affordable and effective faculty development programs are becoming much more apparent.

Substantial numbers of part-time faculty members challenge two-year institutions to provide better systems for evaluation and improvement. Law's (1987) massive study of part-time and full-time instructors found that students rated subject and technical competency about the same for these two groups, but part-timers were rated significantly lower in teaching and evaluating procedures. Two-year colleges can do something to improve performance in these crucial pedagogical areas.

Relationships between goal setting and evaluation and improvement are discussed. Several overview guidelines for faculty evaluation are addressed. A major section focuses on the several inputs that comprise the evaluation of classroom teaching, using research evidence as well as enlightened practices. The major components, such as forms for student ratings of classroom institutions and other elements such as classroom visitation, are analyzed and discussed.

OVERVIEW OF CONTENTS

Chapter 1 discusses ways and means for assessing an institution's climate for evaluating, improving, and judging faculty performance. Past history, current programs, and future needs are crucial elements in charting changes and new programs. Some common elements in the two-year college environment that impact upon evaluating, improving, and judging college performance are given. Developing a proactive and positive evaluation climate is essential to successful evaluation programs.

Chapter 2 focuses on teaching, acknowledging that evaluating faculty requires an awareness that differences among institutions and their academic climates preclude placing emphasis on one evaluative system for all units, programs, and individuals; yet some common evaluation policies and procedures can and should be developed. Also discussed is the importance of having a statement of institutional values as well as operational policies and procedures that are related to evaluation.

Chapter 3 exists in response to the growing impact of part-time faculty on the overall quality of instruction in two-year colleges today. Its goal is to ensure that adjunct instructors receive evaluation and development efforts that are both appropriate and helpful. Included are descriptions of programs from some two-year colleges that address issues inherent with adjunct instructors and work toward maximizing their contributions. Also offered are recommended practices for colleges seeking to improve the process of evaluating, managing, and developing adjunct faculty.

Chapter 4 is about designing faculty evaluation systems. It considers those parts that comprise faculty evaluation systems, focusing upon research findings as well as enlightened practices. Several components are discussed, including reliability and validity of student ratings of classroom performance, and the influences of several factors including class size, grades received, gender, and teacher age. A number of guidelines for developing student rating forms are given. Other major components for faculty evaluation that are discussed include chair evaluation, classroom visitation, college and community service, dean evaluation, personal attributes, professional preparation, and student academic advising. A final section focuses on the ways and means for developing a faculty evaluation system.

Chapter 5 focuses on improving teaching performance and applies to new and experienced faculty members alike. Beginning with several factors that are triggering the current attention to this area, data from the Hopple study discusses the nature and extent of faculty improvement activities, organizational structures for development and funding, funding patterns, and ways for evaluating developmental programs.

Chapter 6 discusses designing and implementing professional improvement programs, including organizational patterns and models. A new, comprehensive model for evaluating institution-wide development and improvement activities is given.

Chapter 7 focuses on making decisions on instructional personnel. Components covered are hiring (both full- and part-time staff members), minority hiring and evaluations, an annual developmental review (ADR), processes and procedures for judging promotion and continuing appointment for staff members, an annual performance review (APR) that uses a weighting system for various components, and making promotion and management decisions on part-time instructors.

Chapter 8 looks into preparing instructors for the next century, outlining seven futures and seven decade needs that will impact significantly upon future thinking and planning for improving faculty performance into the twenty-first century.

An epilogue adds perspective, and a number of appendices provide valuable supplementary materials to the chapters in the text.

THE AUDIENCE

The target audiences for this book include administrators and faculty members in two-year institutions, state-level officials who work with the two-year sector, and those who teach and those students in graduate courses and workshops on two-year programs. These pages also can help faculty members to better understand the elements involved in making better personnel decisions on promotion and continuing appointments for individual faculty members. Also important is gaining a better understanding of the growing body of literature of teaching evaluation and improvement in two-year colleges that provides the basis for further movement in institutional policies and procedures. Comprehensive books that pull together the various pieces are in very short supply.

1

Assessing Your Institution's Climate for Evaluation and Development

The American community college is just over 108 years old, tracing its beginnings to William Rainey Harper, president of the University of Chicago, when he established a junior college in 1892 within the framework of the University of Chicago, using this rationale: "Today only 10 percent of those who finish high school continue their work in college. If the high schools were to provide work for two additional years, at least 40 percent of those finishing the first four years would continue until the end of the sophomore year" (Diener, 1986, pp. 57–58). The conception of the junior college, however, can be traced to Henry Tappan, president of the University of Michigan, who suggested in 1851 that a junior college might be developed to relieve the university of providing general education for young people. The Joliet Junior College was established in 1901 by adding two additional years to the high school program.

From this beginning has developed a vast, sophisticated, practical, and vital segment of the U.S. higher education system. The 1995 fall community college student enrollments totaled 5,440,533, of which 1,961,908 enrolled full-time in public two-year colleges, and 3,478,625 enrolled part-time. Stated another way, 48 percent of all U.S. undergraduates attend community and technical colleges (Phillippe, 1997). The five largest college campuses in the nation include Miami-Dade Community College with over 48,000 students and the Houston Community College system with 47,000 students. Any way one considers the statistics, the two-year sector is an integral part of our nation's higher education system and a vital part of our nation's future.

Vaughan (1995, p. 2) noted that "it is difficult, and perhaps even dangerous, for scholars (and others) to generalize about community colleges in America. Each college has its own unique culture and serves a unique geographic area and clientele. Nevertheless, community colleges in America have much in common, so much so that nationally their development can be viewed as a movement."

The need for effective faculty evaluation and professional development within two-year colleges stems partly from the size of this sector and also from the diversity of its program offerings and its student body. In addition to teaching courses commonly found at four-year colleges, such as biology, history, and nursing, community and technical colleges also offer programs as diverse as travel and tourism, ranch management, law enforcement, dental assisting, and welding. This broad spectrum of program offerings creates the need for a faculty with a considerable diversity of backgrounds and professional preparations.

The diversity in two-year curricula and faculty is exceeded only by the diversity of its students. In addition to well-prepared and motivated students, two-year colleges also enroll large numbers of young people who are academically unprepared for baccalaureate-level work, and others whose immaturity, uncertain interests, or financial conditions make them high-risk students. "Minority student enrollment in community colleges serves approximately 48% of all undergraduate student enrollments each fall term" (Phillippe, 1997, p. 22). Brilliant, self-motivated students can overcome mediocre teaching, but two-year colleges cannot afford this luxury because of the vast array of student backgrounds, interests, and capabilities. Ensuring that faculty members with very divergent backgrounds attain high skill levels of teaching and advising is the prime challenge of faculty evaluation and professional development programs.

SOME COMMON ELEMENTS IN THE TWO-YEAR COLLEGE ENVIRONMENT THAT IMPACT UPON EVALUATION AND DEVELOPMENT

There are several commonalities among two-year colleges across the nation that transcend geographic region, size, and scope.

Community and Technical Colleges Are the Nation's Premier Teaching Institutions

When the national agenda calls for greater emphasis on classroom teaching, the conversation is really referring to the four-year sector because the two-year sector is already there. Two-year college instructional staff members have heavy teaching loads, with four or five sections being the norm and with classes often averaging twenty to forty students. But bigger is not better, and size places additional challenges on learning, teaching, and classroom evaluation. Classroom teaching quality, as judged by student evaluations of two-year and four-year instructional teaching, is quite similar even with the heavier teaching loads in two-year colleges. While teaching is the *raison d'être* of the community college, it is important to remember that "The most successful community college faculty evaluation and performance appraisal systems are those that have included data from a wide range of sources in the evaluation process" (Smith and Barber, 1994, p. 388).

In his comprehensive national study of two-year college faculty evaluation practices, Zitlow (1988, p. 170) used a stratified sample of 333 two-year college chief academic officers (CAOs) who rated 15 variables for their value in assessing *overall* faculty performance. These 15 highest ranked criteria are given in Exhibit 1.1.

Close Working Relationships Among the College and Its Communities' Needs Are Built into the College's Missions and Programming

These relationships have become major aspects of two-year colleges' missions during the past twenty years, and the pace has

Exhibit 1.1
Evaluating Overall Faculty Performance

Individual Items	Mean	Union	Nonunion
1. Classroom Teaching	4.77	4.8	4.8
2. Chair Evaluation	4.05	4.0	4.1
3. College Service	3.61	3.5	3.7
4. Dean Evaluation	3.50	3.4	3.7
5. Personal Attributes	3.48	3.2	3.9
6. Professional Preparation	3.27	3.0	3.6
7. Student Advising	2.91	2.5	3.4
8. Activity in Professional Societies	2.85	2.7	2.9
9. Community Service	2.82	2.7	2.9
10. Professional Presentations	2.50	2.4	2.6
11. Supervision of Internships/Clinicals	2.40	2.3	2.6
12. Length of Service	2.34	2.1	2.6
13. Committee Evaluation	2.19	2.4	1.9
14. Publications	2.12	2.1	2.1
15. Research	1.92	1.9	1.9

5 = Almost always used
4 = Usually used
3 = Sometimes used
2 = Seldom used
1 = Almost never used
National sample of 333 community and technical colleges representing an 83
    percent return rate.

Source: Zitlow, 1988.

accelerated in the last ten years—so much so that some community college leaders are wondering if their colleges are becoming so responsive to community needs and requests that the tail may be wagging the dog. But intense and extensive community and industrial relations, including industrial and business aspects, provide strong mutual benefits that can be expected to increase in the years ahead. Perpetual technological obsolescence afflicts almost all businesses and industries, and their needs often can be met by sympathetic, energetic, and propinquitous two-year colleges. Across the nation, and especially in the more populated states, the majority of businesses and industries can find at least one community/technical college within twenty minutes driving time of their enterprise.

Close community relationships benefit two-year colleges by providing opportunities for additional funding possibilities as well as consulting possibilities for faculty and administrators. These relationships also can contribute to improving faculty instructional performance through their exposure to the world of work. The few faculty members who abuse these opportunities through excessive consulting or outside teaching should not sour these benefits for the vast majority of faculty members.

College advisory committees (CACs) in two-year schools provide unique opportunities for bringing "real world" perspectives and experiences to administrators and staff. The impact of these committees can be useful in program evaluation by providing college teachers with a greater "feel" for and knowledge and understanding of needs and interests of adjacent communities, which they can pass on to their students. Also, these relationships can provide meaningful professional development opportunities for staff and administrators.

The governance processes in two-year colleges feature immediacy and accountability. Chief executive officers (CEOs) must cope effectively and efficiently with monthly board meetings—a phenomenon that is unknown in the governance of four-year colleges. This schedule requires the CEO to have a three-agenda perspective at all times: calling for a clean-up function from last month's board meeting; another series of items related to the upcoming meeting; and longer term projects and studies that will eventually become agenda items for future meetings. Cohen and Brawer (1994, p. 476) noted that "the overriding demand (on administrators) appears to be the need for flexibility in administrative style and approach. All college leaders must have a vision for the institutions they manage. This vision must include a total understanding of the ways their institutions presently function and the ways they could function better."

Curricular and Instructional Flexibility and Adaptability Are Crucial for Modifying Academic Programs to Keep Abreast of New Developments

It has been said within the four-year sector that changing the curriculum is like moving a cemetery; everyone in it is dead, but their friends are not! Two-year colleges are not known for stale curricula, but no school is immune from becoming complacent. Progressive administrators start with a mindset that features questions such as: "Do our program offerings reflect state-of-the-art thinking; how can we cooperate with, or in some cases benevolently co-op, industrial firms into working with us; and are we up-to-date in our equipment and technology?"

Two-Year Colleges Are Becoming Even More Client-Oriented

The current focus on the customer relates closely to current managerial philosophies of W. Edwards Deming and other advocates of something that is generically known as total quality management (TQM) (R. I. Miller, 1996). At no time in our national history has this family of ideas been as prominent as today. Carried to extremes, focusing on the customer could be interpreted as giving the students what they want, but few educators would go that far. More reasonable interpretations call for careful analyses of student interests and needs as valuable inputs into their development and in curricular planning and programming. Other inputs include acceptable performance standards for the profession, new processes and techniques, and individual learning needs among students. On balance, the current focus on the customer is providing a welcome wake-up call for some professors who have been reading from outdated notes and irrelevant materials or who have been overdoing their own thing.

Two-year colleges were client oriented long before Deming's catalytic influence. Admission testing, various types of remediation and special advising, and services for special needs students are a few ways in which two-year colleges have demonstrated sensitivities to the various needs of very diverse student bodies.

Demands for Greater Accountability Have Accentuated the Focus on Evaluation and Development

Societal as well as professional pressures for greater accountability affect two- and four-year institutions alike. While the term "accountability" did not appear in the *Education Index* until June 1970, the concept has been around a long time although defined in other terms such as efficiency and cost effectiveness. Taylor (1911) included efficiency as one of four basic principles of "scientific management" that revolutionized the theory and practice of management in the early twentieth century. Accountability very likely will remain as prominent in the next several years as it was in the 1970s for a number of not-so-mysterious reasons, such as increasingly tight federal and state resources and continuing escalations in human and material costs. Increasing competition for public funds from other public sectors such as health, highways, welfare, and security can be expected as long as the state and national budgets remain frugal.

Society also demands greater personnel accountability, which calls for judging work performance against established/expected norms or standards as well as keeping within acceptable cost ranges. Student evaluation of classroom teaching, chair evaluation of teaching through classroom observation as well as through examination of faculty members' individual teaching portfolios, self-evaluation, and colleague evaluation all can be positive steps toward judging professional performance accountability.

Instructional Staff and Administrators Are Becoming Less Apprehensive About Being Evaluated

Although apprehension over evaluation is decreasing, it is a matter of degree because few individuals really like to be evaluated by others. Institutional cultures in most two-year colleges provide a general acceptance of allowing students, administrators, and colleagues to evaluate classroom teaching as well as other aspects of professional performance.

The ever-changing nature of academic programs and courses has required colleges to become more development prone, yet Hopple's comprehensive study in 1991 found that there is a need for professional development when discrepancies exist between current and desired levels of achievement. Hopple (p. 210) found that the national financial commitment of two-year colleges to professional improvement remained at less than 1 percent of the total institutional budget—which was about the same level of fiscal commitment that Centra found in 1976, using the same research design used by Hopple.

THE QUALITY MANAGEMENT MOVEMENT

Along with the focus on the customer and accountability, the quality management movement that is personified by TQM continues in its various forms. TQM can be defined as the use of management procedures that include intensive involvement of relevant people over a significant period of time with a specific focus or foci, and achieving better performance without significant increases in human and material resources. Indeed, in some cases it means doing better with less. TQM is not a management system as such, although within each targeted area a system can be developed.

What are the relationships between TQM and faculty evaluation and development? Developmental aspects become readily apparent. Faculty members who have participated in TQM projects become more knowledgeable about the various aspects of the college and more sympathetic to a broad array of institutional matters and concerns. The TQM experience can also provide individual renewal through working on institutional matters, and this experience also can result in a more positive attitude toward institutional improvement, which can be helpful in improving academic areas and/or programs. It is an attitude that individuals, by working together intensely and purposefully, can bring about improvements. Thus far, the application of TQM has been very largely confined to the nonacademic or administrative sectors; the academic area can provide new and important challenges.

The *planning-doing-evaluating circle* (Exhibit 1.2) is an important aspect of the quality management movement. The nine functions within the small, inner circle are key elements in evaluating college deans as well as other administrators. This circle has planning, doing (leading and managing), and evaluating as its three component parts, and the application of these components can go forward or backward. One can begin with planning, move to doing (leading and/or managing), then to evaluation; or the circle can begin with doing, moving to evaluating, then to planning. The

Exhibit 1.2
Planning-Doing (Leading-Managing)-Evaluating Model

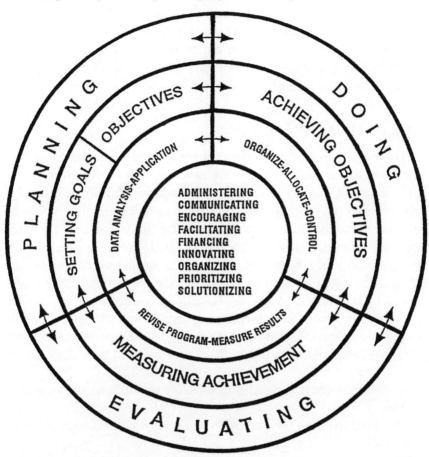

Adapted from McManis and Harvey, 1978.

three elements—planning-doing-evaluating—are inextricably related, and one segment should not be considered without the
other two. In terms of faculty evaluation, short-term planning and
long-term planning are necessary systematic bases for determining future needs and directions.

The manageability of a faculty evaluation system can become
an Achilles heel that causes the system's failure if the management
aspects take too long to complete or are too complicated to com-
prehend readily or are too costly in human and material resources.

The systematic evaluation of an evaluation system often is a for-gotten factor. A committee may take several months to develop a faculty evaluation system without building into the process a sys-tematic plan for evaluating the evaluation system itself. *Ad hoc* and/or impromptu changes in the system may be necessary and desirable, but a systematic evaluation of the evaluation system itself is essential as well.

THE EVALUATION PROCESS

The high percentage of tenured (permanent appointment) fac-ulty within academe nationwide requires that more attention be placed on post-tenure evaluation. The widespread attention being given to accountability, the need to find more effective ways to measure student learning, and curricular outcomes also are forc-ing this consideration. Advocates of such reviews believe that post-tenure evaluations "should be of a formative nature aimed at growth and development, rather than for purposes of repri-mand or revocation of tenure" (Licata and Andrews, 1990, p. 48). In their survey of administrators, Licata and Andrews (1990) posed the following questions for two-year college administrators to ask when looking at the evaluation system in their college:

• Does post-tenure evaluation exist on campus and, if so, for what pur-pose?
• Who participates in the evaluation and with what frequency is it con-ducted?
• What are the outcomes of the evaluation and what problems, if any, are associated with the process?
• Do faculty and administrators view the process as beneficial to ensur-ing institutional quality?
• What suggestions could be rendered for improvement of the process?

Reviewing Evaluation Criteria Is a Prerequisite for Analyzing Post-Tenure Processes

Zitlow (1988, p. 170) studied two-year college evaluation prac-tices, and Licata and Andrews (1990, p. 47) surveyed faculty leaders and community college instruction leaders on desired post-tenure evaluation criteria and they ranked them in this order of importance: classroom effectiveness, courses or curriculum development, contributions to department, campus committee work, innovation in teaching methods, attendance, and reliability. Zitlow also found that classroom effectiveness ranked as the number one criterion that was used in post-tenure evaluation. These findings are not surprising given that the primary expectation of community college faculty is classroom teaching. Licata and Andrews concluded that "respondents clearly do not believe that the criteria used for post-tenure evaluation should differ significantly from the criteria used in pre-tenure evaluation."

Reviewing Problems and Outcomes Associated with the Evaluation Processes Can Help Develop or Revise These Processes

Licata and Andrews also found that 61 percent of administrators indicated that evaluation results were shared with individual faculty members and that a plan for improvement and/or professional growth was established and supported by institutional resources. They also found that 62 percent of the faculty leaders indicated that while evaluations were shared with the faculty members, the faculty members were left to their own devices to correct their weaknesses; therefore, it can be concluded that there may be some disagreement between the faculty and administrators regarding what should be done with evaluation results. This observation could be an important factor when considering the effectiveness of faculty evaluations for improvement. Additional problems found by Licata and Andrews included ineffective implementation of developmental plans, lack of reward systems, inadequately trained evaluators, a need for improved forms, process occurring too frequently, uneven application of criteria, fear of retaliation, lack of guidance following evaluation, failure to segregate achievers, and lack of constructive follow-up as a result of the evaluation process. Licata and Andrews offer suggestions and recommendations for improvements in the evaluation process based upon the respondents' perceptions of what was needed to improve it (see Appendix A).

DEVELOPING A PROACTIVE EVALUATION CLIMATE

What Logan Wilson said in 1942 is equally if not more timely today: "Indeed it is no exaggeration to say that the most critical problem confronted in the social organization of any university is the proper evaluation of faculty services, and giving due recognition through the impartial assignment of status" (p. 112).

Faculty Evaluation Systems Are Designed Primarily to Improve Performance

Some individuals may believe that this guideline is empty rhetoric, contending that the bottom line is the use of faculty evaluation for making academic promotion and tenure decisions. If this guideline is indeed empty rhetoric, then the institution is at risk of finding that cynicism about helping individuals improve is the best way to turn the creative minds of faculty members toward finding ways to subtly thwart or circumvent the system.

The previous statement does not deny the importance of summative evaluation for making personnel decisions, but if the "system" has reasonable credibility among institutional staff members, then negative faculty evaluations can be seen as signals for improving performance of individuals who are performing below par. Alternately, the evaluations can be seen as a way of improving teaching performance by replacing those teachers who have poor present performance and who are judged as having little reasonable expectations for future improvement. This concept also does not deny the importance of terminating the services of staff members who do not meet institutional standards or who find themselves in obsolete fields.

Staff Evaluation and Development Programs Are Linked with a General Statement of Institutional Values

Linkages between staff evaluation programs and institutional values signify that selected institutional values are taken seriously enough to be used in determining the degree of progress that has been made toward them. Community colleges accept the logic and the fact of teaching evaluation but often have not linked institutional values with the evaluation program.

One statement of values was developed by Lethbridge Community College (LCC), in Lethbridge, Alberta, Canada. Started in 1957, LCC is the oldest community college in Canada. Its institutional statement of values focuses on human development, excellence, accessibility, communication, and accountability. A series of evaluation and development policies and procedures were designed to move the institution toward achieving these values.

Miami-Dade Community College's statement of "Teaching/Learning Values" contains these seven values:

I.   Miami-Dade Community College values learning.

II. Miami-Dade Community College values change to meet educational needs and to improve learning.

III. Miami-Dade Community College values access while maintaining quality.

IV. Miami-Dade Community College values diversity in order to broaden understanding and learning.

V.   Miami-Dade Community College values individuals.

VI. Miami-Dade Community College values a systematic approach to decision-making.

VII. Miami-Dade Community College values partnership with the community. (Miami-Dade Community College, 1988. See Appendix B for measurable descriptors for each value.)

Your College Has an Instructional Staff Evaluation System

While every college has staff evaluation, an evaluation *system* is much less common. Most often a system is not a system but a series of parts that are very loosely integrated, if at all. A "system" can be defined as a number of components, such as student ratings, classroom observation, self-evaluation (portfolio), and colleague evaluation that are linked together synergistically so the whole is greater than the sum of the parts. (These components will be discussed in greater detail in later chapters.) The system also includes articulated information and instruction about administering and using the various components of the system, and about the uses of the various inputs in the promotion, tenure, and annual review processes.

Faculty Evaluation Results Are Used Significantly in Making Decisions About Classroom Performance

What should be a self-evident truth is, in reality, sometimes more window dressing than substance. Two-year colleges will not admit to taking faculty evaluation lightly or using it as a facade, but sometimes the reality can be quite different. A poorly designed, poorly administered, or politically contrived system would be enough reason to take lightly the evaluation process and its results.

Staff Evaluation and Improvement Programs Are Organizationally and Operationally Linked

For example, the college official who has prime organizational responsibility for the teacher evaluation system should be in close liaison with the one who directs and/or coordinates the teacher development program, and in some cases it may be the same person. These one or two individuals should have regularly scheduled meetings with the chief instructional officer. The difficulties involved in making such linkages can tell the participants something about possible gaps in either or both dimensions.

Faculty Evaluation Is Done on a Regular Schedule— for Everyone

There is no logic or equity in excluding senior instructors from the same classroom teaching evaluation that is applied to junior, nonpermanent appointment teachers. Some differences do and should arise in the extent of evaluation. For example, instructors who are not on permanent appointment may have a somewhat more extensive evaluation, but some evaluation feedback, such as from students and from the chairperson, should be for everyone and for every course.

An Annual Development Review (ADR) and an Annual Performance Review (APR) Are Conducted Each Year

One or two scheduled annual meetings between each instructor and his/her immediate supervisor should be held annually. These thirty-minute to one-hour meetings should focus on performance evaluation and on professional development over the past year and should take a serious look ahead. The results of the meeting should be summarized in a written report. Details about the ADR and the APR can be found in Chapter 6.

Some Balance Is Needed Between Institutional Needs and Individual Interests

The nature of the balance between institutional and individual needs may be more or less in flux. In times of economic scarcity, institutional needs become more important *vis-à-vis* individual interests. These may be classified as "worth" and "merit" decisions, saying that the worth of the individual to the institution is primarily an institution-level decision, whereas the *merit* of the individual is primarily a professional judgment based on his or her academic credentials and performance and should therefore be determined primarily by professional colleagues. The key point is that administrators remain aware of the distinction between worth and merit during the faculty evaluation processes.

Evaluation Is an Integral Part of the Planning-Doing (Leading-Managing)-Evaluating Circle

Efficient and effective evaluation systems cannot be developed without substantial planning or without considering carefully the human and material costs in managing and leading the system. In other words, evaluation systems should always be considered in planning and managerial aspects (refer back to Exhibit 1.2).

Institutional Climate Is Conducive to Developing, Sustaining, or Modifying the Evaluation System

Climate problems may be due to low faculty and/or administrative morale, mutual mistrust, fiscal crises, or lethargic leadership. Assessments of true causes and reasons for problems may be difficult, and these problems could be the part of the iceberg that is beneath the surface.

The Senior Administrative Staff Provides Sustained, Helpful, and Sincere Support to Evaluation in General and Faculty Evaluation in Particular

A reality check on this point can be made by checking out how and how often administrators are evaluated. The saying "what is good for the goose is good for the gander" supports the notion that faculty members have every right to expect a known and systematic evaluation plan to be in place for every level of administration. The intention of the system should be the same for administrators as for faculty members, which is to improve, not terminate, people. Not only will a professionally sound and comprehensive administrative system improve performance and morale in that sector; it will help faculty members accept faculty evaluation. It is important, however, that the administrator evaluation system is comprehensive and has "teeth."

Evaluators Are Qualified to Evaluate Faculty

Arreola (1995) observed that "true objectivity in a faculty evaluation system is a myth" (p. 2), explaining that the goals need to control the impact of the subjectivity. A prominent potential source of subjectivity lies with the chairperson, and realizing that merely holding the title does not ensure competence is a starting point for bringing effective and efficient leadership to the process.

Because of the diversity of transfer technical degree programs within the two-year college sector, a diverse range of expertise in the art and skills of evaluation can exist among department chair and/or coordinators. This diversity can result in inconsistent evaluation from department to department. One example is a technical faculty member who objected to what he considered to be a low evaluation. The chair tried to assure the teacher that his performance was strong and that the evaluation was very positive. "But look at these check marks in the Meets Expectations column," came the teacher's reply. "These suggest a minimal level of performance. I wouldn't hire someone with this evaluation." But the chair replied, "Well, if someone is meeting *my* expectations, he's doing one hell of a job." This chair is probably defining "meets expectations" in a different way than most chairs across the college, which results in his faculty evaluations being more severe than the same performance would have earned from another evaluator.

In the same college, another chair gave all nine full-time faculty within his department scores of fours and fives (on a five-point scale) in every category. Was the faculty that exemplary? No; the chair admitted years later that he did not know what to look for and gave everyone the benefit of the doubt. Still another chair felt so inadequate in the role of evaluator that she procrastinated scheduling the classroom observations until it was too late. At that point, she could then give only glowing assessments because she could not defend any unfavorable comment in lieu of first-hand observation.

An assumption may be made that chairs are inherently objective, impartial, knowledgeable, and consistent across the institution, but the inability of chairs to accurately evaluate teaching performance can create legal problems for the college. In one instance, a two-year college professor was being considered for tenure; however, the tenure committee found itself in an uncomfortable position because, despite the individual's history of unprofessional classroom behavior, the chairperson had consistently given him very favorable evaluations. The dichotomy developed for two primary reasons: (a) the chairperson highly valued diversity of teaching styles, and (b) she had hired him and was unwilling to admit to having made a mistake. Just as a chain is only as strong as its weakest link, faculty evaluation systems depend upon the evaluators to be knowledgeable, unbiased, and consistent.

Finally, Expect Some Opposition to Changes in Faculty Evaluation Policies and Procedures

And you will not be disappointed! Arreola (1995, p. 6) raised these common faculty and administrator resistances to changes (improvements) in faculty evaluation and developmental plans in two-year colleges.

Stage 1. Disdainful denial

Stage 2. Hostile resistance

Stage 3. Apparent acquiescence

Stage 4. Attempt to scuttle

Stage 5. Grudging acceptance

Earlier, Astin (1976, pp. 75–85) wrote about games that academic people in four-year institutions may play in their efforts to subtly or not so subtly sabotage or not come to grips with new ideas and programs. These games include rationalization, passing the buck, obfuscation, recitation, and displacement and projection, including undue caution. It is not very likely that these games are entirely the preserve of four-year people.

CONCLUSION

The future of two-year colleges is both challenging and important. As noted by Cohen (1997, p. 1), "Projecting the future for the community colleges of the early twenty-first century involves projecting the future for the nation in general; its demographics, economy, and public attitudes. . . . Community colleges will play a role in this process similar to that which they have developed over much of this century: pre-baccalaureate, occupational, remedial, and adult education, provided to a broad spectrum of the local population."

2

Focus on Teaching

During the early twenty-first century, community colleges can be expected to encounter opportunities for achievement that may be mistaken as chronic problems or looming disasters. National, state, and local changes in levels of tax support; the movement to upgrade standards; student resistance to tuition increases; census demographics; and the clamor for enhanced accountability will affect all community colleges. Success in these sometimes inhospitable environments will depend very largely on the quality of the individual community college program, and program quality is directly dependent on the talent, flexibility, commitment, and effectiveness of the college's faculty. On these scores, the community colleges often will be in a better position to compete than the four-year sector.

Quality of teaching always has been controlled by a community college's institutional *culture*. Borrowed from the social sciences and popularized in the business literature, "culture" has been defined in a number of ways. In his study of a suburban community college, Kempner (1991, p. 221) "looked for cohesive elements and patterns of behavior from faculty, administrators, and students that helped define the mission and teaching function of the college."

Excellent information on two-year college organizational culture was gained through the classic 1989 Community College Effectiveness Study—a national survey conducted by the Community

College Consortium, which had 2,115 replies from executive administrators, mid-level administrators, research-assessment coordinators, and faculty at 136 community colleges. In analyzing these data, Peterson and White (1992) underscored critical aspects of everyday operations as viewed through the college culture lens:

The culture of each college affects student success. The unique patterns of practice, ritualistic behaviors, and symbolic expressions comprise a context that informs how students, faculty, and administrators work and interact. In some instances, the culture of a technical institute may support career success but inhibit transfer to a four-year college or university. Conversely, a college that actively promotes the value of its transfer mission may make its vocational students and staff feel like second-class citizens.

In recent years there have been some negative public perceptions of the community college culture. Its critics contend that it is an undisciplined sector that tolerates a high dropout rate as it channels unprepared minorities into vocational areas, lacks effective performance in "transfer and baccalaureate degree completion," and concentrates on remedial and developmental experiences at the expense of the "integrity" of the curricula.

Such criticisms have important implications for the decisive importance of the community college faculty. As summarized by Alfred and Linder (1990, pp. 24–31): "The basic problem is one of institutional effectiveness promoted through teaching and learning. . . . Community colleges are under pressure to make fundamental changes in curricula and strategies for teaching and learning to produce students with cognitive skills that meet the requirements of baccalaureate degree granting institutions, business and industry, and others." Decisions on how best to utilize and to evaluate community college faculty members are inevitably linked with an understanding of the purposes served by the college.

Most two-year schools offer both transfer and technical programs of study; the latter can be either associate degree or shorter certificate curricula including disciplines as diverse as welding, piano tuning, meat cutting, respiratory therapy, ranch management, and forestry. In matters of faculty promotion, evaluation criteria need to be sensitive to differences among departments, otherwise a single campus-wide system may favor nontechnical faculty by developing a system that favors their strengths. For example, in some technical areas such as graphic arts, it is difficult to find schools that award graduate degrees, thereby placing faculty in those areas at a disadvantage. In such an instance, alternative measures of subject expertise need to be devised. For example, instead of looking at the highest attained degree, the highest level of licensing may be a more valid criterion. In programs that are closely monitored by external agencies, such as aviation maintenance which is monitored by the Federal Aviation Administration, course outcomes already may be so prescribed that there is much less opportunity for a professor to alter the course curriculum and thereby earn credit toward promotion.

Faculty promotion systems in many divisions and schools have achieved a desirable level of equity among their programs by allowing divisions to reflect the realities of their situations within the structure of institutional guidelines. Evaluating faculty can require an acknowledgment that the differences among academic disciplines preclude the application of a single method of assessing performance. For example, in areas such as English, history, and the social sciences, faculty promotion is commonly tied to the attainment of an advanced degree, but in technical areas expertise is measured by licenses or certification. In addition, the duties can vary to reflect the nature of students enrolled in that discipline, the industry being served, or the nature of the job itself. Student advising duties can vary between degree-granting departments and those departments that do not offer majors.

When Columbus State Community College in Columbus, Ohio, established a system for faculty ranking, the accompanying promotion system consisted of several stages of review. To attain promotion, each candidate submitted a portfolio that was evaluated by the academic department, a division promotion review committee, the division dean, a college-wide promotion review committee, the academic vice president, and the president. These levels of assessment reflected an understanding that the four academic divisions—health and human services, business and public service, engineering technologies, and arts and sciences—were not identical in the expectations of their faculty members. To allow for these differences, the college recognized licensure and certification, as well as academic degrees, as evidence of professional preparation. Also, each division created its own manual to assist candidates in the preparation of the portfolio and to interpret or to define certain provisions in the college-wide policy. For example, the college required that candidates demonstrate "exemplary performance" in a prescribed number of professional areas such as scholarship, curriculum design, and student advising, but the definition of exemplary performance could vary among the divisions. In short, with the diversity of academic programs at two-year colleges, one size does not fit all.

WHO ARE THE FACULTY?

Gilbert Highet (1950, 1989, p. 235) wrote that "we all teach and learn, all our lives." The teaching function in two-year colleges has tended to be associated almost exclusively with the classroom, although community colleges have accorded faculty status to a wide range of personnel. In addition to full-time teaching instructors, the ranks of community college instructional staff can also include part-time or adjunct instructors, librarians, staff in student personnel services, and the occasional college administrator teaching a course during the academic year. Librarians, for example, seek to achieve recognition as faculty and have long asserted their teaching functions. Raufman, Williams, and Colby (1990, p. 103) reviewed documents and journal articles in the Educational Resources Information Center (ERIC) data base addressing the involvement of two-year college learning resource centers (LRCs) in teaching and learning. They found that these

centers at community colleges are approaching their instructional responsibilities in a number of ways. Most LRCs offer some form of library orientation, and all target their collection-development policies to support their colleagues' instructional programs. Over the past ten years, many LRCs have increased their computer resources and become active partners in audio-visual services, computer-assisted instruction, and computer literacy programs.

Lowry (1993, p. 165) in a 1990 national survey found that for librarians in two-year colleges, 69 percent had faculty status, 27 percent had professional status, 2.3 percent had academic status, and 1.7 percent had civil service status. Two-year colleges that have awarded faculty status to nonteaching professionals need to develop assessment approaches that take into account the unique duties of the category.

Teaching Faculty

The typical two-year college faculty member is an experienced teacher, middle-aged, with a master's degree. He or she belongs to national professional associations but has seldom published. The long-range goal is to remain in the position, and the preferred teaching style is a combination of lecture and discussion. But organizational conditions in 1997 continued to keep some two-year faculty members from achieving their professional potentials, in much the same ways that were spelled out in a major 1988 report by the American Association of Community and Junior Colleges (AACJC) entitled, *Building Communities: A Vision for a New Century: A Report of the Commission on the Future of the Community College*. This report stated that community college teachers often feel overextended, typically teaching at least five sections per semester. Classes, especially in basic subjects, often are too large and preparation time is too short for faculty to feel effective. On too many campuses there is a feeling of burnout and fatigue among the institutional staff, and a loss of vitality that weakens the quality of teaching.

Further, community college teachers, especially in career and technical programs, often do not have the fiscal support they need to keep abreast of their dynamic professions, and many feel isolated and out of touch with colleagues in their fields. "Sixty-three percent of the community college faculty in a national survey rated the intellectual environment at their institution as 'fair' or 'poor.' In a climate such as this, teaching effectiveness is diminished and the potential for excellence is lost" (AACJC, 1988, pp. 11–20). There is no evidence that these general conditions have dramatically improved in many two-year colleges in recent years, although, in fairness, some community colleges have developed exemplary faculty evaluation and developmental programs.

The 1988 AACJC study also found that large general education classes, usually for economic reasons, "[increase] the student drop out rate" (p. 2), which is also true today. The willingness of administrators to cancel sections of literature courses, for example, with less than optimum enrollment may lower faculty morale. Evaluating a frustrated general studies teacher without being able to offer hope of improved classroom teaching environment will do little to improve teaching effectiveness. But administrators will succeed who believe that evaluation is an integral part of a college-wide plan to improve student outcomes and who seek to involve the faculty in efforts to develop the necessary conditions for substantially upgrading the academic program and the morale of those who teach in it. In a study of faculty job satisfaction among two-year colleges in the midwest, Finley (1991) found that there was a wide range of job satisfaction on issues involving faculty evaluation; however, administrators who believe that evaluation is an integral part of a college-wide plan to improve student outcomes and who seek to involve the faculty in developing and evaluating these efforts can put in place the necessary conditions for substantially upgrading the academic program and the morale of those who teach in it.

What Do We Want the Faculty to Do?

The faculty is *the* major human capital of the community college, which underscores the *primary* duty of the two-year college administration in recruiting and deploying faculty to enhance the college mission and to achieve its objectives. Momentarily putting aside the varied privileges and unevenness of faculty senates and college faculty unions, it remains both the prerogative and the duty of the college administration to decide how best to utilize its instructional resources. Such deployment is most effective for a community college when made in the context of a well-designed and implemented plan of evaluation and development. In their community college effectiveness study, Alfred, Peterson, and White (1992, pp. 29–33) outlined what they saw as the optimum future for effective community colleges and their faculties:

Effective community colleges will implement systems for continuous environmental scanning, performance assessment, and planning at the service unit and academic department levels. In the process, faculty roles and workloads will change. Tomorrow's faculty members will do more than teach. They will forecast market conditions, plan and evaluate curricula, conduct research on student outcomes, build marketing and recruitment plans, lobby private-sector markets for resources, and perform other management functions as necessary to improve program performance. Collective bargaining contracts will need to be rewritten to simultaneously change the nature of faculty workload and maintain continuity in faculty and administrator roles.

Also, data from the community college effectiveness study indicated that effective community colleges have an overriding interest in student success. Alfred, Peterson, and White noted that "three important characteristics differentiate high performing community colleges from mediocre ones: (1) reputation for quality, distinctiveness and innovation, (2) flexible strategies for delivering programs and services, and (3) systems for evaluating and improving performance" (1992, pp. 10–14).

FACULTY EVALUATION OVERVIEW

Evaluation Needs to Be Based upon Articulated Values

Purposes and programs need to be related to a carefully developed values statement. What are the institutional values? This is a question commonly absent in most institutional statements about evaluations and organizational purposes. As previously noted, the values statement developed by Lethbridge Community College consisted of human development, excellence, accessibility, communication, and accountability. Miami-Dade Community College's "Statement of Faculty Excellence" (see Appendix B) emphasizes dedication, challenges, the integration of knowledge and teaching, respect for diversity, and organization.

Some institutional instructional improvement and evaluation plans skip over a values statement either by oversight or by considering that the basic values of honesty, hard work, individualization, fairness, free enterprise, helping others, and obeying the law are "givens," and therefore it is not really necessary to have a statement about them. Still, colleges that tackle these values questions generally find that the conversations are intensive, conflicting, sometimes emotional, and specifically inclusive, yet an agreed-upon statement does allow an umbrella that should thereafter be reflected in policy and operational statements. Also, if this statement is consistent with operational policies and procedures, it can provide additional legal protection.

Evaluation Should Be Purposeful

Those administrations who begin, continue, or extend faculty evaluation systems should not disregard "means and ends" questions. For example, citing the extensive Southern Regional Education Board Survey of administrators at 536 colleges and universities, Ratcliff (1984) noted that

this study found no evidence that institutions with systematic faculty evaluation plans had characteristics of superior teaching and learning when compared to those colleges without such plans. While institutions with evaluation systems did gather information useful in personnel decision-making, the survey did not indicate that such information was regularly used for personnel decisions.

Those surveyed institutions that did not utilize evaluation data for personnel decisions had not fully determined the reasons for assessing faculty performance in the first place. They had not answered the "why" question—a crucial necessity for any college program. Would the results of a similar study today find substantial differences?

Evaluation Should Be Manageable

An effective and efficient management system for handling and processing the evaluation data is essential for effective and credible results. Sometimes, in an effort to please too many constituencies, evaluation systems come to resemble more an elephant than a race horse! Along with an effort to please many constituencies, the final plan can be administratively top-heavy in terms of its operation. If the plan is too labor intensive, it may be too cumbersome in its operations and thereby undermine its decision-reaching time line, which can diminish its credibility and effectiveness. Some faculty evaluation systems have fallen under their own bureaucratic weight.

The System Should Be Perceived as Fair

Faculty members may not agree with some evaluation decisions, but they should not be able to say that the system is substantially unfair and gain general agreement from key faculty members. Faculty members are prone to try to beat a disliked and/or distrusted system. To make the fairest decisions and to make them hold, credibility is a crucial element.

EVALUATING TEACHING

In their extensive study, Hammons and Barnsley (1996) concluded that there was very little valid research on the characteristics of effective community college teaching; that a shift in focus had occurred from the teacher-centered characteristics (those looking into teacher's personalities) to the more student-oriented characteristics; the community college literature on this subject was sparse; and there was very little consensus on the characteristics of the effective community college teacher. (See Exhibit 2.1.)

To learn how two-year college faculty are being evaluated, the Zitlow study (1988) used a survey instrument that was developed and used initially by the American Council on Education in 1967, and later used by John Centra for his *Determining Faculty Effectiveness* in 1979. The Zitlow study is based upon a national, stratified sample of chief instructional officers at community and technical colleges. The usable return rate of 83 percent represented 333 community colleges, or about one-fifth of the nation's total number.

Exhibit 2.2 identifies the major items that two-year colleges use for evaluating teaching performance. Each item can provide insight into overall performance, but each one also has limitations if used alone or if given excessive weight. When several data sources are used in the appraisal, the weakness of one source can be offset by the strength of others. Also, the use of multiple sources can enhance both the perceived and the actual fairness and acceptance of personnel decisions.

Exhibit 2.1
**Top Ten Ranking Characteristics of Effective Community College
Teachers from 1920 to 1989**

Characteristic	Number of times mentioned in that decade						
	1920–1930	*1940*	*1950*	*1960*	*1970*	*1980*	*Total*
1. Is student-oriented—interested in students	3	2	2	6	12	16	41
2. Has a thorough knowledge of subject matter	1	3	4	7	13	3	31
3. Uses a variety of teaching methods	1	2	1	4	10	7	25
4. Possesses good communication skills—explains effectively	0	1	1	6	9	6	23
5. Motivates—inspires students	0	4	3	3	4	7	21
6. Is organized—plans well	0	1	2	3	7	8	21
7. Has an inborn capacity—is dedicated to, enjoys teaching	2	1	2	3	10	2	20
8. Is enthusiastic	0	0	3	6	4	6	19
9. Has broad scholarship	0	3	2	4	2	1	12
10. Keeps up-to-date in field	1	1	1	0	6	2	11

Source: Hammons and Barnsley, 1996.

Zitlow found that chair evaluations, classroom visits, and systematic student ratings were the three most frequently used
sources in the evaluation of faculty classroom teaching performance. All three sources have mean scores in the 4.0 range, indi-
cating that they are extensively used in two-year institutions.
Course materials, dean evaluations, and formal self-evaluations
with scores of approximately 3.5 were frequently used also.

The significant use of classroom visits in appraising teaching in
two-year colleges is a definite contrast to findings for four-year
institutions. Seldin (1980; 1984) found that classroom visits ranked
tenth on a list of fifteen factors used in evaluating faculty teaching

Exhibit 2.2
Evaluating Faculty Teaching Performance

Individual Items	Average	Union	Nonunion
	M	M	M
1. Chair Evaluation	4.04	3.9	4.2
2. Classroom Visits	3.95	4.2	3.7
3. Student Ratings	3.91	3.7	4.1
4. Course Materials	3.20	3.4	3.6
5. Dean Evaluation	3.50	3.5	3.7
6. Formal Self-evaluation	3.36	3.2	3.6
7. Student Opinions	2.81	2.7	3.0
8. Committee Evaluation	2.06	2.4	1.6
9. Student Examination Performance	1.94	1.7	2.3
10. Scholarship	1.91	2.0	1.8
11. Enrollment in Elective Courses	1.63	1.6	1.7

Sample: Includes 333 technical and community colleges, with an 83 percent return rate from the original sample.
Rating scale:
5 = Almost always used
4 = Usually used
3 = Sometimes used
2 = Seldom used
1 = Almost never used

Source: Zitlow, 1988, p. 82.

in four-year colleges, and Traylor (1992) found that classroom visitation ranked ninth in a list of twelve criteria for evaluating classroom teaching.

Variances in the administrative structures of two-year and four-year colleges account for some of the differences in the use of classroom visits as a source of evaluation data. Permanent deans and chairpersons are quite common in two-year institutions, whereas their counterparts in four-year colleges often serve specified terms before rotating back into the faculty. Due to the permanence of their roles as well as the traditional use of classroom observation, administrators in two-year colleges are more prone to make classroom visits to evaluate faculty members they supervise. Also, the unionization of approximately 40 percent of the nation's two-year college faculty leaves the evaluation functions to chairs and deans because the traditional union axiom, "brothers

cannot evaluate brothers," often excludes faculty classroom observation for summative purposes.

Evaluating Faculty Scholarship

Faculty scholarship in the Zitlow study included research,
publications, and professional presentations, and these three components were further divided into the individual items of professional presentations, articles in professional journals, books as sole
author, articles in quality journals, monographs, books as a junior
author, and editor of a journal. Zitlow found that CAO responses
to these individual items indicated very little support for including faculty scholarship as a criterion for evaluating teaching. This
item was rated as very infrequently used regardless of union
status or level of institution size. All eight individual items in this
criterion factor had mean ratings of 2.0 and 2.4, which placed them
in the "seldom used" category.

The three components of faculty scholarship—publications, research, and professional presentation—were also included among
the fifteen individual items for evaluating *overall performance*, and
all three components were rated as seldom used. Research and
publications were the least used of the fifteen items with means
of 1.9 and 2.1, while professional presentations ranked tenth with
a mean rating of 2.5.

The fact that scholarship has a very low priority in overall criteria for appraising faculty performance should not be construed
as saying that scholarship is necessarily unimportant. In an important book by the late Ernest Boyer, *Scholarship Reconsidered*, his
broader definition of scholarship can enhance teaching by encouraging more interesting and meaningful materials for both the
teacher and the taught. The Commission on the Future of Community Colleges wrote about the necessity of encouraging some
aspects of scholarship within the community college faculty, noting: "In addition to the scholarship of *discovering* knowledge,
through research, it is also important to recognize the scholarship
of *integrating* knowledge, through curriculum development, the
scholarship of *applying* knowledge, through service, and above all,
the scholarship of *presenting* knowledge, through effective teach-

ing. These are areas of vital importance to community colleges" (AACJC, 1988, pp. 26–34).

Vaughan (1989, p. 9) noted that research in the traditional sense is "not important at all for 95 percent of faculty members but it is important to be scholars." In other words, the canons of scholarship, which include carefully gathering authentic data, dispassionate analyses, and reasoned conclusions based upon the available data, should be sought by all teachers.

To foster faculty scholarship to the advantage of the college and its service objectives, expectations for scholarly activities can be helpful. Parilla (1986, pp. 4–5) reported on Montgomery County, Maryland, Community College's program to foster faculty scholarship. According to the institution's *College Policies and Procedures Manual*, faculty were given support:

1. To conduct or complete the scholarship and writing for a paper or publication.
2. To prepare or complete a work of scholarly synthesis or opinion.
3. To participate in a performing arts activity, such as directing a professional community play or conducting an orchestra.
4. To create or complete an artistic work such as a painting or musical composition.
5. To perform discipline-related work in a public or private setting as a non-paid consultant or intern.
6. To hold a major office in a discipline-related local, state, or national professional organization.
7. To develop knowledge of the state of the art developments in the technologies areas by participating in non-paid work in a public or private setting.
8. To update teaching and professional competence through the reading of an extensive bibliography of works at the cutting edge of the discipline, as part of a preplanned program.

Adopting or adapting programs from other community colleges, including the support/designation of a college development office to assist scholars in meeting their scholarship expectations, can help prepare faculty members to undertake meaningful scholarship efforts. In any case, a planned approach to faculty research, grounded in a college's student-centered goals, can both enhance assessment and increase program effectiveness. Collaborative efforts that recognize shared faculty and administrative concerns for teaching, advising, and scholarship are essential to successful programs.

MAINTAINING PERSPECTIVE

Finally, evaluation needs always to be kept in perspective. When is enough evaluation enough? Planning-doing (leading-managing)-evaluating are inextricably linked. Evaluation should be primarily for improvement, and if faculty and staff believe otherwise, then administrators and influential teachers need to seek the reasons for this belief. Businesses, athletic teams, and colleges learn from both their failures and successes if they are to improve. Evaluation for performance improvement is important and not just for younger faculty members who are working toward permanent appointment but for everyone—staff and administrators alike.

3

Improving Part-Time Teaching

Two-year college enrollments continue to grow at a substantial rate, with 86 percent of the colleges increasing enrollments in the last ten years, and nearly 60 percent having major enrollment increases (American Council on Education, *Campus Trends*, 1996). To supplement staff, save money, avoid excessive commitment to contract personnel, and employ individuals to teach in specialized areas, the proportion of part-time faculty has grown dramatically in most colleges, and this growth is expected to increase at least as fast in the foreseeable future. In addition, part-time faculty are available to be groomed for full-time positions that may be expected in the future.

Prudent use of adjuncts in metropolitan area colleges, with their greater abundance of qualified people, can serve as a buffer for enrollment shifts and new instructional needs. In one midwest urban community college, the English department has a 12 to 72 ratio between full-time and part-time faculty, the physical and biological sciences department has a 15 to 80 ratio, and the mathematics department's ratio is 10 to 52. During a recent fall term, 70 of the 77 sections of a beginning algebra course were staffed by part-time instructors. Clearly, the sheer number of instructors to be evaluated places a large burden on the departments to ensure that each instructor is evaluated comprehensively and fairly. Since part-time instructors have a crucial role in fulfilling the college's instructional mission, they should not be shortchanged in the development and evaluation processes. Academic departments with large numbers of adjunct faculty may find that the task is too much for one chairperson, and therefore they select one or more full-time faculty to assist in this process with some release time made available to facilitate their assistance. Union agreements in some colleges, however, may not permit this practice.

NOTEWORTHY PROGRAMS

A number of colleges have developed programs to enhance the contributions of their adjunct faculty.

Kellogg Community College

Kellogg Community College in Battle Creek, Michigan, provides all part-time faculty members with a handbook designed to familiarize them with KCC policy and procedures, including basic information and sample forms for many of the everyday processes and procedures such as drop/adds. The handbook also discusses course outlines, attendance and grading policies, and other basic information for getting started as a part-time faculty member at Kellogg.

Monroe County Community College

Monroe County Community College in Monroe, Michigan, uses approximately 65 full-time and 165 to 170 part-time faculty members and offers new adjunct faculty a part-time faculty workshop that is held on Saturday mornings. The program allows participants to choose from concurrent sessions and concludes with a luncheon. Their part-time faculty handbook covers basic information about the campus, the college's processes and procedures, a section entitled "Teaching Tips" that includes an examination of the special needs of adult learners, the different styles of content presentation, and uses of audiovisual materials.

Hocking Technical College

Hocking Technical College in Nelsonville, Ohio, has a program for part-time instructional improvement, which started in the

1970s, called the Quality Instruction Program (QIP). The college hires many part-time faculty directly from industry with no college teaching experience. Several administrators saw the need to orient newly hired faculty members both to instructional processes, such as writing syllabi and evaluating student performance, and to the college and its systems. At first, college officials were unsure whether to mandate participation of all new faculty because some new employees had extensive prior teaching experience. Ultimately the college decided to encourage participation by paying a small additional hourly wage to those who completed the program. Now the college has made participation a condition of employment for all faculty without prior teaching experience and for those holding contracts exceeding 50 percent of full-time employment.

The QIP is a four-day seminar that is held prior to the start of fall quarter. Participants are given a brief history of the college, its mission, its student-oriented philosophy, an instructional position job description, and sample formats for course outlines and course syllabi. Participants also develop lesson plans for each of the two in-class observations scheduled during the first quarter of teaching, provide two evaluation tools appropriate to the material to be presented, attend preobservation conferences with a teacher educator, successfully present two lessons during the quarter while being observed by a teacher educator, participate in a one-hour follow-up to observation conference, complete a journal about their teaching experiences, and participate in weekly one-hour seminars.

The Adjunct Institute

Developmental activities for adjunct faculty have become commonplace, but all two-year colleges need to ask themselves, "How can we do a better job of helping our adjunct teachers?" Money and time can be real impediments, although the outstanding staff development programs have found that such expenditures need not be expensive. One successful program for adjunct development is The Adjunct Institute at Burlington County Community College, Pemberton, New Jersey. Their Adjunct Faculty Institute, as described by McCadden (1994, pp. 1, 6), is held twice annually, usually on the first three Saturdays of October and February. The program consists of five three-hour sessions that run from 9:00 A.M. until noon, and from 1:00 P.M. until 4:00 P.M. The initial session focuses on the information in the college catalog, particularly the college's grading policies; the second session involves a tour of the campus as well as presentations by selected Board of Trustee members; the third session revolves around the placement, registration, and counseling services at the college; the fourth session deals with the art of teaching; and a fifth session focuses on teaching minority students. One of the secrets of the program, according to McCadden, "is that the college rewards adjuncts for their participation. We reward them by paying them $20 per session for attending. Also, once they complete the course they receive a certificate of accomplishment."

Skilled adjunct faculty are of immeasurable value to colleges, and some students report that their best instructors are part-timers. Yet if not monitored properly they can create problems, especially if they are hired near the start of the term to teach added sections and do not receive adequate orientation. Inadequate orientation can create several types of problems:

1. Part-time instructors who work full-time in other noncollegiate jobs may not always have a solid sense of their new duties. For example, full-time faculty whose classes follow those of adjunct faculty have found copies of tests lying near the podium.

2. Those who have primary careers that are outside of education may not take their teaching seriously enough.

3. Those who work under contracts of one quarter or one semester may believe that their continued employment is dependent upon favorable student evaluations. To this end, some faculty may inflate student grades in an effort to avoid complaints and to enhance their evaluations. However, the research on student ratings indicates that enhancing student grades does not enhance student ratings of the classroom instruction.

To neutralize these possible problems, the college can have in place a system that requires each part-time instructor to be observed and evaluated early enough into the term to identify areas to be strengthened. Graber (1997, p. 3) found that having new adjuncts visit classes of experienced teachers can be quite useful provided visits are planned carefully with follow-up conversations.

MENTORING

Mentoring has become a popular concept in recent years, and it is something that incurs little opposition. However, it often has had little analysis.

One study identified four kinds of mentors. The *friend* interacts with the mentee socially, providing advice about people and helping with personal problems. The *career guide* promotes the development of the mentee's research, inclusion in a network of colleagues, and his or her professional visibility. The *information source* provides information about formal and informal expectations for promotion and tenure, publication outlets, and committee work. Finally, the *intellectual guide* promotes an equal relationship, collaborates with the mentee on research or publications, and provides constructive criticism and feedback (Sands *et al.*, 1991, p. 174).

In their book-length discussion of mentoring in an industrial setting, Murray and Owen (1991, pp. 13–14) offered some useful information that can be adapted by two-year colleges. Their lists of possible activities for the mentor and for the protégé can be helpful. The literature base for mentoring in two-year college literature is quite sparse as compared to the materials available for industry.

Some mentor roles include the following:

- Act as a source of information on the mission and goals of the organization.
- Provide insight into the organization's philosophy of human resource development.
- Tutor specific skills, effective behavior, and how to function in the organization.
- Give feedback on observed performances.
- Coach activities that will add to experience and skill development.
- Serve as confidant in times of personal crises and problems.
- Assist the protégé in plotting a career path.

- Meet with the protégé at agreed time intervals for feedback and planning.
- Agree to a nonfault conclusion of the mentoring relationship when (for any reason) the time is right.
- Maintain the integrity of the relationship between the protégé and the natural boss.

Some *protégé* roles involve the following:

- Willingness to assume responsibility for one's own growth and development.
- Assessing one's potential to succeed at one or more levels above the present position in the organization.
- Ability to perform in more than one skill area.
- Seeking challenging assignments and new responsibilities.
- Being receptive to feedback and coaching.

Based upon the belief that the cost of a faculty-to-faculty mentoring program is insignificant compared to the cost of replacing unproductive faculty, St. Clair (1994, p. 31) suggested these criteria for developing a mentoring program:

1. Design of the mentoring component would be the primary responsibility of the faculty development coordinator. It would be an extension of an already existing program.
2. Any full-time or part-time faculty member could serve as a mentor. The only criteria for becoming a mentor would be willingness to serve and the background and experience to provide the service.
3. Numerous mentors would be recruited to serve any mentee who has a need. No one would feel solely committed to any one person.
4. Mentoring would be optional for both mentors and mentees. Those volunteering to be mentors would be compensated by a decrease in committee appointments or duties other than teaching.
5. The mentor would share teaching resources, be available to observe the mentee teaching, be observed by the mentee, share positive and negative experiences, and insight into the community college teaching and learning culture, and serve as a role model of an effective teacher.
6. The mentee would consult with the mentor on teaching techniques, seek guidance on the development of one's teaching, and solicit in-

formation about the teaching and learning culture at the community college.

7. Evaluation of the entire program would include collection of data on reactions to the mentoring program as well as comparisons of pre- and post-mentoring student evaluations of an instructor's teaching.

These data would be analyzed with the help of the academic research staff.

STUDENT ADVISING

An important part of professional improvement systems is advising part-time and full-time students. In comparison with many other two-year instructional matters, there is very little research and literature about these matters. Two successful advising practices are outlined here. One is reported by Paris (1996) at Coffeyville Community College in Kansas. This "early warning system" is a simple, user-friendly computer program that is accessible through e-mail. Faculty use the system to document student performance, track progress, note student absences and low test scores, and intervene if necessary. The system is efficient and eliminates considerable paperwork. Benefits to the college are saving many students from probation and increasing student retention, from 48 percent at Coffeyville Community College in 1989 to 74 percent in 1995. The increase between fall 1994 and fall 1996 was 86 percent, and the overall grade point average of "at risk" students rose appreciably.

A second faculty advisor system is described by Ramos (1996) in the Houston Community College System. With just two counselors to serve 2,500 students at one of the system's colleges, there was concern about adequately advising students regarding academic transfer programs. The college implemented an academic faculty advisement system in which faculty would donate time during fall, spring, and summer semesters. Each faculty member made available one hour weekly to advise academic transfer students. Advising hours were counted toward fulfillment of contractually required office hours. To ensure a fair work load, each department head submitted an equal number of faculty advisors, available for both day and evening counseling. A modified walk-in advising system was created. For several weeks, beginning just after midsemester in the spring, students were encouraged to meet with faculty advisors on a walk-in basis. In order to make students aware of the newly available counseling, a list of advisors, their academic disciplines, and time availability was publicized throughout the campus—in classrooms, in the library, in the student lounge, on bulletin boards, and in faculty, counselor, and administrative offices.

Benefits from this program were that the college was able to offer more services to students; productivity of department heads, faculty, and counselors increased; student retention improved; and enrollment increased in academic programs. Classroom teaching performances by adjunct teachers as compared with full-time teachers showed very little differences in teaching ratings by their students.

What does the research say about possible differences in teaching performance based upon full- or part-time employment? A comprehensive study of comparative teaching competence of part-time and full-time two-year teachers was completed by Law (1987) and involved teachers from six community and six technical colleges in Ohio. Using Educational Testing Services, Modified Student Instructional Report (MSIR), and 256 part- and full-time teachers, he found that "part-time and full-time faculty were comparable in most of the dimensions of teaching effectiveness as perceived by the students" (p. 188). There were no statistically significant differences between part-time and full-time faculty as perceived by their students in the areas of course organization and planning, faculty/student interaction, communication, knowledge of subject, and enthusiasm of the instructor.

With respect to their examination and test practices, however, full-time faculty were rated significantly more effective than the part-time faculty. Students also said that examinations given by the full-timers reflected more closely the important aspects of the courses. Students perceived no significant differences between the part-time and full-time faculty in their overall teaching effectiveness, whether the faculty members were from community or technical colleges or from small, medium, or large-size colleges (p. 187). Two other studies by Grymes (1976) and Lolley (1980) also found that there were no significant differences in teaching effectiveness between part-time and full-time instructors.

If the teaching effectiveness of part-time and full-time instructors is about even, why bother? In the interests of constantly seeking to improve, however, Law's study does indicate that additional assistance given to part-time instructors in examination and test practices would be helpful. In this activity full-time instructors rate significantly higher than part-timers. Among the predictor variables, Law found that "institutional involvement" was the best predictor of teaching effectiveness for part-time teachers, and "teaching experience" was the best predictor of teaching effectiveness for full-time teachers.

Roueche, Roueche, and Milliron, in their article entitled "Identifying the Strangers: Exploring Part-Time Faculty Integration in American Community Colleges" (1996, p. 39), concluded that "a disturbing finding from this study is that few college administrators are aggressively and systemically directing their colleges' efforts toward integrating part-time faculty." The article includes a useful "part-time faculty integration model."

The hiring, evaluation, retention, and permanent appointment policies, procedures, and processes for part-time faculty should be reviewed periodically. Constructing and revising definitions of criteria for making instructional personnel decisions can be time consuming and complex, but they are important to institutional effectiveness and efficiency, to orderly and equitable decision making, and to good staff and administrator morale.

CONCLUSION

Researching their book on part-time instructors, Gappa and Leslie (1993, pp. 234+) included visits to eighteen colleges and universities, five of which were two-year colleges with multiple campuses including Miami-Dade in Florida and Cuyahoga Community College in Ohio. Their list of forty-three recommended practices can assist in gaining better control over the evaluation, management, and development of part-time faculty employment:

1. Develop goals for the use of part-time faculty that are based on the educational mission of the college or university.

2. Include the use of part-time faculty in the overall faculty staffing plan.

3. Consult part-time faculty during development of the faculty staffing plan.

4. Assign responsibility, delegate authority, develop policies and guidelines, and review and monitor adherence to the policy.

5. Systematically and routinely gather and use accurate and timely data on part-time faculty for decision-making purposes.

6. Periodically survey part-time faculty for additional information about their perceptions of the conditions under which they work, their satisfaction with their employment, and other concerns or interests.

7. Assess the benefits and short- and long-term costs of employing part-time faculty.

8. Review and evaluate the faculty staffing plan on a regular basis.

9. Establish a campus-wide representative body to give advice on part-time faculty employment policies.

10. Publish part-time faculty employment policies in the faculty manual and distribute them to all department chairs and faculty, especially part-time faculty.

11. Make department chairs responsible for implementing part-time faculty employment policies consistently.

12. Offer a range of employment options for part-time faculty.

13. Provide for part-time tenure. "By 'part-time tenure' we mean tenure in a position that is clearly understood to have a specified time base that is less than full-time" (p. 250).

14. Provide security and due-process rights for part-timers with seniority and records of effective performance.

15. Appoint continuing part-time instructors for more extended periods.

16. Establish career tracks that provide rewards and incentives for long-term service and/or high achievement.

17. Identify qualifications for part-time faculty that are legitimately related to the job requirements.

18. Recruit, select, and hire part-time faculty proactively.

19. Diversify the part-time faculty pool through affirmative action.

20. Provide timely and early notification of appointments to part-time positions.

21. Develop a salary scale for part-time faculty.

22. Ensure consistency of compensation practices for part-timers within departments and institutions.

23. Set standards for progression through the salary scale.

24. Provide benefits to continuing part-time faculty.

25. Develop objective performance criteria and procedures for evaluating part-time faculty and use the results as the basis for decisions about reappointment.

26. Provide support service to part-time faculty.

27. Communicate the message that part-time faculty are important to the institution.

28. Give department chairs responsibility and incentives to supervise part-time faculty.

29. Orient department chairs to good supervisory practice.

30. Invite part-time faculty to share their perceptions of effective supervisory practice at department training sessions.

31. Use teams of experienced faculty (full- and part-time) to develop new faculty members' teaching skills.

32. Provide faculty mentors to inexperienced part-time faculty.

33. Engage full- and part-time faculty in course coordination.

34. Involve part-time faculty in the assessment of student learning.

35. Appoint part-time faculty to committees.

36. Involve part-time faculty in informal talk.

37. Invite part-time faculty to social events.

38. Publicly recognize part-time faculty for their achievements and contributions.

39. Orient part-time faculty to the institution and to the expectations the institution has for them.

40. Conduct frequent workshops on good teaching practices.

41. Provide in-service professional development opportunities for part-time faculty.

42. Provide incentives for good performance.

43. Use teaching evaluations to help part-time faculty improve.

4

Designing and Implementing Faculty Evaluation Systems

Evaluation is a means toward providing better education for students, improving academic performance, and making better personnel decisions. Including both formative and summative dimensions, evaluation is designed primarily to assist in the ongoing processes of improving teaching and learning. Because faculty members carry this titular responsibility it is important that they be fully involved in developing policies and procedures to improve these processes.

Significant changes and improvements in faculty evaluation have taken place over the past decade. Systematic use of faculty evaluation has increased significantly, and the use of faculty development programs is increasing also although more slowly. Using a greater number of qualitative performance measures in making academic personnel decisions is evident although there is an optimal number of criteria that can be used and still have the system managed efficiently. Functional "systems" for faculty evaluation are being developed, survey instruments for appraising various kinds of performance have improved significantly, and court cases generally have resulted in better and more equitable uses of faculty evaluation systems.

OBJECTIVES FOR FACULTY EVALUATION

A statement of objectives for a faculty evaluation system should be developed if one does not already exist. The following objectives are suggested:

1. To establish an evaluation process that can be used to identify faculty strengths and weaknesses as a fundamental step toward improving professional effectiveness.
2. To develop a framework within which professional growth and development is encouraged.
3. To create a process within which the quality of instruction may be improved in the interest of student success and the enhancement of student retention.
4. To make personnel decisions on promotion, continuing appointment, and merit based upon professionally sound evaluation systems.

MAJOR COMPONENTS OF OVERALL FACULTY EVALUATION

The Zitlow study (1988) evaluated all major phases of two-year faculty and, as mentioned earlier, used almost the same criteria that were developed and used initially by the American Council on Education in 1967 and later by Centra for his Educational Testing Service study in 1979. The Zitlow study used a stratified national sample of technical and community colleges with data from 333 technical and community colleges, with a usable return rate of 83 percent.

In developing a faculty evaluation system, it is not necessary or desirable to use all of the evaluative criteria that are given in Centra's and Zitlow's studies. The seven *overall* criteria of greatest national prominence found among the fifteen criteria that were used in the Zitlow study were: (1) classroom teaching, 4.77; (2) chair evaluation, 4.05; (3) college service, including committees, 3.61; (4) dean evaluation, 3.50; (5) personal attributes (cooperation, attitude), 3.48; (6) professional preparation (degrees, licenses), 3.27; and (7) student academic advising, 2.91. (See Exhibit 1.1 for the full list of fifteen items.)

Classroom Teaching

Zitlow's study found that the six most important (out of fifteen) criteria for evaluating *teaching* were:

1. Chair evaluation (discussed on page 4a as no. 2 in overall faculty performance evaluation)   4.04
2. Classroom visits   3.95
3. Systematic student ratings   3.91
4. Course syllabi   3.62
5. Dean evaluation   3.50
6. Formal self-evaluation   3.36

The following section discusses common research findings about validity and reliability of student ratings, some general principles for developing instruments for student rating of classroom teaching, distributing and collecting the student rating forms, and processing and using these summaries.

Reliability and Validity of Student Evaluations of Teaching Effectiveness

Marsh and Bailey (1993, p. 122) noted that student evaluation of teaching effectiveness (SETE) forms are probably "the most thoroughly studied of all forms of personnel evaluation, and one of the best in terms of being supported by empirical research." A synopsis of the comprehensive study of four-year schools by Marsh and Bailey (p. 17) concluded:

SETEs are (a) multidimensional; (b) reliable and stable; (c) primarily a function of the instructor who teaches a course rather than of the course that is taught; (d) relatively valid against a variety of indicators of effective teaching; (e) relatively unaffected by a variety of variables hypothesized as potential biases to the ratings; and (f) seen to be useful by faculty as feedback about their teaching, by students for use in course selection, by administrators for use in personnel decisions, and by research.

Most summaries of research on evaluation of teaching have reached very similar conclusions. Costin and associates (1971),

McKeachie and associates (1986), Miller (1972, 1987), Centra (1993), and others have found that student evaluations of teaching that use multiple choice questionnaires can provide valid and reliable indicators of the quality of classroom teaching.

Student evaluation of classroom teaching by a standardized student evaluation form is the top-ranked criterion in studies of elements involved in evaluating teaching effectiveness. Zitlow's study found a 3.91 rating on a five-point scale. Teaching is defined as those activities associated with the design and delivery of course material to students. For purposes of evaluation, the instructional role included, but is not limited to: content expertise; instructional design skills such as syllabi, test design, supplementary materials, and grading procedures; laboratory preparation and maintenance, where applicable; pedagogical (teaching) skills, including enthusiasm, organization, delivery, and communication skills; evaluation of students through tests, reports, projects, and other methods; student-related activities, such as regularly scheduled and kept office hours, and academic and career advising; and rapport with students.

The inclusion of student evaluation of faculty is questioned by some professors who doubt that students are mature enough to make fair and valid assessments of classroom teaching. Several writings have pointed out factors that allegedly could influence student ratings and thereby render them less valid. Among these suspected factors are class size, grades received, gender, teacher personality, and teacher age.

Class size. A common perception holds that instructors of large classes are at a disadvantage because these classes are unpopular with students and the large class size hinders learning. Research indicates either no support of this contention or a modest relationship, which is "not enough to use large classes as an excuse for low ratings" (Gleason, 1986, p. 12). Other findings support this earlier generalization (Weimer, 1990).

Grades received. It seems reasonable to assume that students receiving low grades might blame this on the teacher. Over 300 research studies have focused on this issue, and the large majority of them conclude that there is not a high correlation between grades received and teacher ratings. Aleamoni (1981) found that of the twenty-eight studies that reported positive relationships, median correlation was approximately 0.14. Similarly, Centra (1979, p. 32) found a low (0.20) correlation between grades received and student ratings of classroom teaching. In their summary of the research on student grade expectations, Braskamp and Ory (1994, p. 178) found that "students expecting high grades in a course give higher ratings than do students expecting low grades."

Gender. Most studies have found no *significant* differences in faculty ratings based upon the gender of either the students or the teacher (Aleamoni, 1981; Centra, 1979, 1993). In their survey of the literature on factors influencing student ratings of course or instructor, Braskamp and Ory (1994, pp. 177–178) concluded that "no significant relationships exist between gender of instructor and his or her overall evaluation, although ratings do slightly favor women instructors." In terms of gender of students, they found that "gender of student and overall evaluation of instructors are not related although students tend to rate same-sex instructors slightly higher," but the differences were far from being statistically significant.

Teacher personality. Most studies have found that teacher personality variables are not prominent predictors of teacher ratings. Gleason (1986) observed that students are capable of distinguishing between personal popularity and teaching effectiveness, and Aleamoni (1976) found that students are able to evaluate friendly teachers accurately by reporting shortcomings such as poor organization and ineffective communication while also recognizing strengths such as warmth and a sense of humor. The literature survey by Miller (1987a) and Braskamp and Ory (1994) concluded instructor warmth and enthusiasm are generally, but not in a statistically significant way, related to instructor personality, but no meaningful and consistent relationships exist between the personality characteristics of the students and their ratings.

Age and teaching effectiveness. With the uncapping of the retirement age on January 1, 1994, college teachers have no mandatory retirement by federal law. This law raised more seriously than previously the question of teaching effectiveness and age. Some empirical evidence is available and has been summarized in a comprehensive report by Kinney and Smith (1992, pp. 292–302). They concluded:

The empirical research in this study has revealed that there is no significant relationship between student evaluations of teaching effectiveness and age among the active tenured faculty, and that relationship varies structurally across the broad disciplines of humanities, social sciences, and physical and biological sciences. It appears that student evaluations of teaching effectiveness actually improve for tenured professors in the humanities and the social sciences as they approach the current mandatory retirement age [then 65 years], though, in the social sciences, these evaluations first decline between the early forties and the mid-sixties. It is only in the physical and biological sciences that evaluations decline as faculty approach the current mandatory retirement age. In each instance, however, the impact of age on teaching effectiveness is quite small. Concerns that a serious decline in the quality of higher education because of a deterioration in teaching competence will accompany the uncapping of mandatory retirement for tenured faculty appear to be unfounded.

Earlier summaries of research on age and teaching found mixed results. Centra (1979) found that faculty with more than twenty years of teaching received lower ratings than those with twelve years of experience. Similarly, Centra and Creech (1976) found that faculty receive the highest ratings between the third and twelfth years of their careers. More recently, from a related perspective, research studies report mixed findings when looking at the relationship between teacher rating and faculty rank. Gage (1970) and Walker (1969) found a positive correlation between higher rank and higher ratings, but more recent research reported no significant correlation (Aleamoni and Thomas, 1980; Linsky and Straus, 1975). A more recent survey of the literature on "years teaching" by Braskamp and Ory (1994, p. 177) relied heavily upon the landmark study on this subject by Feldman (1986, p. 198), which concluded that "rank, age, and years of experience are generally unrelated to student ratings."

A caveat: The bulk of the extensive body of research supports the position that student evaluations of faculty performance are acceptably valid. However, most of the basic research on the topics covered in this summary is pre-1990, and very little of it has focused on two-year colleges. Until studies are performed within the two-year sector that provide contrary findings, the validity levels of two-year students as evaluators of faculty performance are assumed to be very similar to those for the four-year students.

Some General Principles for Developing Instruments for
Student Rating of Classroom Teaching

The questions on the survey instrument should ask things and include activities that are relevant to the students' classroom experiences. A class of 20 to 25 students spends between 700 and 800 teacher-watcher hours per instructor per semester; therefore, if the evaluation form asks students the right and relevant questions, they can be expected to make fair and perceptive judgments.

Students are knowledgeable about class matters relating to class organization and management, pedagogical methods, fairness, teacher's interest in the student's success, and in normative or comparative questions. Students usually are asked about the teacher's knowledge of subject, but the most authoritative answers to this question will come from colleagues and line administrators and not from students.

The questionnaire should be simply worded, and each question should represent only one evaluation point. "Pet" and extraneous questions should be avoided. Brevity, while sometimes not an instructor's forte, should be a guide for evaluation forms. There is no research evidence that equates the quality of the questionnaire to the length of the number of questions.

Psychologists and others may try some theoretical approaches such as changing the scale for every other item by alternating the use of positively and negatively worded questions. Students do not buy into such tricks and may either not answer the questions or answer them in their own way.

The form should be unsigned by students. This is a must.

The data processing system for collating the questionnaire data should be simple and fast with a turnaround time of about two weeks to get the survey results so they may be used for developmental purposes. A form for student rating of *classroom teaching* is included as Exhibit 4.1.

Distributing and Gathering the Student Rating Forms

It is important to use a systematic and consistent approach to distributing and gathering the student rating forms in order to

Exhibit 4.1
Student Rating of Classroom Teaching

INSTRUCTOR _____ DATE _____

COURSE _____ ACADEMIC TERM _____

   Thoughtful student appraisal can help improve teaching and learning effectiveness, and this questionnaire is designed for that purpose. Your instructor also is interested in your personal comments; therefore, please respond to the questions on the reverse side of this form, adding any comments you may have. Do not place any means of personal identification on this form and confidentiality will be maintained. Thank you for your assistance.

Directions: Please mark the number of the response that best describes your opinion about each of the following statements. If you "don't know," mark "X". Place your numerical rating in the blank space before each question.

Highest			Middle			Lowest		No Opinion
7	6	5	4	3	2	1		X

_____ 1. Course assignments related closely to the course objectives.

_____ 2. Class sessions were effectively planned.

_____ 3. Class time was efficiently used.

_____ 4. Teaching methods and techniques were conducive to meaningful learning.

_____ 5. Course work assignments and deadlines were reasonable.

_____ 6. Instructor had mastery of course content.

_____ 7. Instructor was interested in the subject.

_____ 8. Instructor respected differing points of view.

_____ 9. Instructor created an environment which fostered student involvement; she/he encouraged students to ask questions and/or participate in class discussions.

_____ 10. Instructor provided alternate ideas to those presented in course materials.

_____ 11. Instructor demonstrated a professional interest in helping students.

_____ 12. Instructor's grading policies and procedures for this course were fair.

The instructor or unit may insert several additional items in the following spaces:

_____ 13. _____

_____ 14. _____

_____ 15. Considering all the above items, what is your overall rating of this instructor in teaching this course?

Exhibit 4.1 (*continued*)

_____ 16. In comparison with other instructors in the academic unit, how would you rate this instructor?

(NOTE: Your *handwritten responses* to the following questions will not be seen by the instructor; rather, he/she will see a typed copy of them.)

A. What did you like most about the instruction of this course?

B. What did you like least about the instruction of this course?

C. Would you recommend any changes? If yes, what would you recommend?

D. Other comments.

Thank you for your assistance.

gain optimal human and material cost savings as well as to maximize consistency and fairness in collating the data. The following system is recommended:

A. Faculty evaluation forms are completed by every student in every class during the week *preceding* final examinations.

B. Class instructor designates one student to deliver the forms to the assigned place.

C. The instructor distributes the forms, without comment, then sits at the front of the room in a nondescriptive way while students complete their forms. Sitting allows a lower profile and therefore a somewhat less threatening one.

D. Students place their unsigned evaluation forms, backside up, on a table away from the instructor.

E. A designated student places all forms in a large brown envelope, seals the envelope in the presence of the instructor, and delivers it to the appropriate office accompanied by the instructor.

F. All student rating forms are processed at the same time. All comments on the back of the survey form should be typed by a neutral third party if possible, and may be returned later in some cases. Confidentiality of comments is important to the students.

G. A data analysis system provides quick and easily interpretable feedback of summaries of the evaluation instrument. This is easier said than done, but it is a crucial step.

H. Turning the student responses into data analysis reports for each instructor and the appropriate administrators should take no more than two weeks. This short turnaround time provides data early enough to be useful for the next term.

I. The data analysis reports should be sent simultaneously to the instructor and the supervisor.

Using the Forms

If the forms are processed within a fairly short time (about two weeks), they can be more useful for instructor self-analyses as well as for chairs and others who have developmental as well as personnel decision responsibilities. Care always should be taken in using and interpreting the tabulated results. For example, the number of student raters can have an impact upon reliability. Centra (1973) found that if five raters were used, the reliability coefficient for overall teacher rating was 0.65; for ten raters, 0.78; for twenty-five raters, 0.90; and for fifty raters, 0.95.

Chair Evaluation

What Peltason (1982, p. xi) said about chairs in four-year institutions applies also to two-year colleges: "An institution can run for a long time with an inept president but not for long with inept chairpersons." A great deal of literature has been developed on the nature and function of the chair position for four-year institutions, but two-year institutions have a very meager literature data base on this subject.

Major national studies of two- and four-year colleges have consistently found that the chair's role in the evaluation of teaching ranks first or second in importance. The modus operandi for the chair's office in matters of evaluation should include these factors:

• Know historically the general expectations for the chair position at your institution and the more specific expectations for your instructional area.

- Know specifically the roles of the chair in evaluation of teaching as well as improving faculty performances. Read the files carefully and know thoroughly your institutional policies and procedures as well as any additional ones for your unit.
- See that all institutional policies and procedures on faculty evaluation are carefully followed. When in doubt, ask the appropriate academic officer.
- Make on-time delivery of all paperwork, remembering that processing of cumulative reports has the speed of the slowest or last report.

The major teaching evaluation roles of chairpersons call for providing leadership in selecting new faculty members, then providing them with continuing professional assistance; working toward more efficient and effective policies and procedures for formative and summative evaluations; making evaluations for promotion and continuing appointments; working with problem cases, including burn-out and/or phase-out; and being a persistently strong advocate for better faculty teaching and student learning.

Classroom visitation in two-year colleges is the most common criterion that chairs use in evaluating classroom teaching. Between 35 and 40 percent of all two-year college instructors work in unionized institutions, and because most union contracts do not permit "brothers to evaluate brothers," classroom visitations by nonunion administrators or their designators become a necessity.

The secondary school literature on classroom observation is more fully developed than the post-secondary literature. McGreal (1983, p. 97) outlined four tenets for either formative or summative observational evaluation of teaching in the public school that are relevant to two-year institutions.

- The reliability and usefulness of classroom observation is related to the amount and type of information supervisors have prior to the observation.
- The narrower the focus that supervisors use in observing classrooms, the more able they will be to describe accurately the events related to that focus.
- The impact of observational data on supervisor-teacher relationships and on the teacher's willingness to fully participate in an instructional improvement activity is directly related to the way the data are recorded during observation as well as how those data are used subsequently.

• The impact of observational data on supervisor-teacher relationships and on the teacher's willingness to fully participate in an instructional improvement activity is directly related to the way feedback is presented to the teacher.

Steps and Processes for Making Classroom Visitations

The processes selected and used for the visitation are the key to its effectiveness. The following visitation process may seem detailed and comprehensive, but it is fair as well as legally defensible.

A. Classroom observer(s) are selected. If the college is unionized, then administrators may be the only ones available who can do the visit. The observer may be a chair, dean, division head, or a designee. Two observers are better than one; however, limitations in human resources usually mean that not more than one observer can be used.

B. The visitation time is mutually set through a meeting or telephone conversation between the classroom teacher and the observer. The "pop-in" unannounced visit is not recommended for several reasons. The pop-in class period may be one which is primarily a review session or the teacher may be discussing the results of an examination or doing other things that are not directly related to teaching.

The mutually agreed-upon class period will allow instructors to put forth their best lectures, which is professionally preferable to the unannounced visit which smacks of "trying to catch the teacher doing something wrong." On this point, one nationally prominent two-year college had its designated administrators conduct unannounced classroom visits during each spring quarter. During this quarter some instructors—probably those who are apprehensive about their status—carried along a spare lecture or two for such unannounced visits. Generally known to the students who were willing participants in the charade, they would slip the "ringer" lecture unobtrusively upon the podium to enhance the teaching performance evaluation! Subsequently this college has dropped the unannounced visit.

C. For the scheduled classroom visit, the instructor supplies, in advance, a course syllabus as well as a lesson plan for the observation day, which allows the observer to see how those class activities fit into the overall course plan.

D. What to observe? One observer might prefer a participative style of teaching that involves the students often, seeking to have them come up with answers rather than to be told them. Or the observer may favor more lecturing, believing that a reasoned and rational lecture can draw forth appropriate and directed student responses. If the observer prefers to teach primarily by telling and is observing a teacher who is doing the opposite, he may give that teacher a somewhat lower mark. To help minimize possibilities of subconscious biases, a common observation rating form should be used by each observer. The questions essentially are the same ones that another set of observers—the students—use to evaluate classroom teaching. Because both the students and the visiting observers are watching the same individual with the purpose of rating the quality of teaching, it is desirable that essentially the same instrument be used by both groups. A copy of a classroom visitation form for the outside *observers* is included in Appendix D, and a copy of the Self-Evaluation of Teaching form is given in Appendix E, which should be completed by the *classroom instructor* and shared with the class observer.

E. The observer completes the classroom visitation form and written report within five working days. Such a deadline is desirable to avoid unintended delays in finishing these reports and perhaps creating a log jam of reports. The observer simultaneously sends a second copy of the evaluation report to the teacher who was observed.

It is very desirable that a scheduled meeting about the observation report take place between the observer and the teacher although lack of time may be the primary deterrent to this meeting. Generally, both the observer's and the teacher's comments are passed on to the chair and dean for additional consultation and/ or finalization.

The processes involved in conducting fair and professionally sound classroom visitations are not simple or quick, and the importance of making reasoned and fair observations and conclusions also can be complex and sensitive.

College Service

This activity including committees ranked third (3.61) in the overall rankings of items used in the evaluation of overall faculty performance (see Exhibit 1.1).

Evaluating college service most likely is done by the chair and/ or the dean who makes some subjective judgments about the quality of the college service. The Zitlow study (1988, p. 107) used nine criteria for evaluating faculty *college service* performance, with these criteria and their mean ratings on a five-point scale.

1. College-wide committee   3.4
2. Development committee   3.2
3. Department administrative duties   3.0
4. Academic advising   2.9
5. Advisor for student organization   2.5
6. Undesirable courses   2.2
7. Campus symposia   2.1
8. Student recruiting   2.1
9. Nonacademic counseling   1.9

Community service ranked ninth (2.82) in Zitlow's list of fifteen items used for evaluating overall faculty performance. The four criteria for community service received these ratings:

1. Volunteer service   2.7
2. Advice to business (consulting)   2.6
3. Training/development programs   2.6
4. Community presentations   2.6

Evaluation systems for *faculty service* evaluation should include self-evaluation and chair evaluation. The rating form for self-evaluation of teaching (Appendix E) can be helpful as a checklist of useful activities as well as providing blank spaces for additional comments.

Appendix F is an evaluation form for appraising teaching materials that can be used by the chair and/or a committee as well as for self-evaluation of the use of teaching materials such as text-books, manuals, and computer software.

Evaluation of community service can be more complicated than evaluating college service in that it should include a short report and an evaluation from the employer in addition to a report by the involved faculty member as well by the chair. This process may seem cumbersome, yet current processes for evaluating college and community services often are nonprocesses with very little accountability or paperwork.

How much consulting should there be? With increasing opportunities for community and industrial consulting, what can be done with the few individuals who abuse this privilege? First, one needs to establish what constitutes "abuse." Usually this very murky line is drawn when outside interests infringe excessively or noticeably on college responsibilities. How much consulting should be expected or allowed? It depends upon the individual, the academic area, the institution, and its geographical location, but one day per week is an accepted rule of thumb, provided that it does not interfere with assigned or expected professional responsibilities (Boyer and Lewis, 1985). How does consulting impact upon regular professional responsibilities? In their research summary, Boyer and Lewis (1985, p. v) found: "The available evidence clearly suggests that those faculty who do consult are, on the average, at least as active in their other faculty roles as their peers who do not consult."

Dean Evaluation

Deans in two-year colleges often serve more varied roles than do their counterparts in four-year colleges. They need to anticipate problem evaluation cases as far in advance as possible, and they do not like surprises. Deans often try to keep an arm's length away from the ongoing, operational processes of evaluation in order to facilitate more independent judgments based on the candidate's file, review of both "worth" of the individual and his or her academic area to the mission of the college, and the "merit" of the individual's performance. Deans have valuable checks-and-balances roles in the evaluation processes, which help to ensure that the system is fair to the individual in the context of instructional goals and objectives as well as the unit's more particular needs.

Personal Attributes (Cooperation, Attitude)

These general criteria are important in making academic personnel decisions, yet they can be very difficult ones to judge. Human relations are significant in all walks of life including academe where freedom of speech and the right to differ are at the heart of the college enterprise. Both personality and performance enter significantly into collegiate decision making, but the ways in which these decisions are made are important.

Exhibit 4.2 is a form for evaluating these sensitive matters. "Faculty service and relations" has five items that can somewhat objectify the personal attribute components of acceptance of college assignments, attitude, cooperation, performance on college assignments, and professional behavior as it relates to professional activities and nature of the institution. Currently, decisions on personal attributes often are made almost exclusively upon episodic bases, impressions, or hearsay—hardly sound bases for serious decision making. A form can help professionalize these decisions.

Professional Preparation (Degrees, Licenses)

This criterion is usually spelled out in the faculty handbook, and in many cases a step system of salary increments is closely related to academic degrees and/or certificates or licensure.

Student Academic Advising

This criterion in Hopple's study of faculty development in two-year colleges (1991) was ranked number seven in overall performance criteria, but institutions with enrollments under 4,000 students and nonunionized institutions placed more importance on this activity. In both evaluating overall faculty performance and evaluating college service, nonunionized faculties placed significantly greater importance on academic student advising (3.4)

Exhibit 4.2
Faculty Service and Relations Evaluation

Name of Teacher ————————————— Date ——————

Appraiser ————————————— Title ——————

Directions: Please give your judgment about the quality and quantity of the individual's campus professional service and relations.

Additional questions may be added as items 9 and 10.

Highest			Middle			Lowest		No Opinion
7	6	5	4	3	2	1		X

_____ 1. Acceptance of college assignments. The faculty member accepts college assignments willingly.

_____ 2. He/she volunteers occasionally.

_____ 3. The faculty member acts in the best interests of the department and the college.

_____ 4. A constructive attitude is taken toward human relations and personnel problems.

_____ 5. The faculty member assists colleageus and others with their professional activities and problems.

_____ 6. A positive and helpful attitude is taken toward colleagues.

_____ 7. The individual acts responsibly toward the goals and nature of the institution.

_____ 8. How would you rate the individual's overall performance level on college related activities and assignments?

_____ 9. On professional behavior as it relates to professional activities and the goals and nature of the institution.

_____ 10. ————————————————————————

_____ 11. ————————————————————————

_____ 12. Considering all of these items, what is your overall rating of this instructor in this course?

Describe specific faculty assignments and services: (Use additional space if necessary.)

————————————————————————————

————————————————————————————

Comments: ——————————————————————

————————————————————————————

————————————————————————————

as compared with those with faculty unions (2.5). The quality of student advising is directly related to student retention.

Hopple found significant differences for academic advising between two-year institutions with enrollments under 4,000 students, which placed more emphasis on faculty responsibility for advising students, and those with enrollments greater than 4,000, which placed less emphasis on student advising. The CAOs generally believed that student advising is fairly important, ranking it seventh in the list of fifteen items; however, greater attention on academic advising in all two-year colleges could be a useful thrust toward achieving better retention rates.

Student advising is a "numbers game" in many two-year colleges. With heavy teaching assignments and large classes, faculty members often do not have professional time to do the type of personalized advising that most of them want to do. Some colleges have moved toward advising processes that use a cadre of faculty members who work primarily as advisors; other colleges give lighter teaching loads to teachers who become part-time advisors. In the developmental (remedial) area, two-year colleges have done some of their best advising, and many success stories can be cited.

A Plan for Campus-wide Evaluation of Student Advising

The following low-cost and high-dividend evaluation process of student advising can help one understand and improve institution-wide student advising. Immediately before every quarter or semester, or at least once every academic year, the CAO calls a two-hour meeting of all deans and chairs that focuses on advising for the upcoming term or year. Many small, but potentially large, problems can be addressed ahead of time and thereby diminish potentially negative fallout.

Individual departments can support the student advising function in several ways. First, they can administer questionnaires that supply information about the students' high school preparation, employment work loads, current class schedules, distance traveled from home, and academic goals. With this data, high-risk students can be identified in time for appropriate advising. Second, cider and doughnut sessions can facilitate informal interactions between students and faculty advisors, thereby establishing a positive rapport that encourages students to seek out their advisors when their problems are still small ones.

Departments should seek flexibility in assigning advisors to students. Too often this is done only by some arbitrary system such as the first letter of a student's last name (e.g., A-F go to Mrs. Nelson). A more practical system for nonresidential campuses may begin in this fashion but also allow students to see the advisors whose office hours are compatible with the students' class and work schedules; students cannot get help from advisors they cannot reach. Finally, the advising function often is not covered thoroughly during faculty orientation or in-service sessions, with the result that faculty can have varying views of their roles and provide widely varying approaches and advice to students. Departments need to define what is expected of faculty advisors and supply the informational support that ensures a more uniform level of performance.

Students Should Evaluate Advising

Faculty advising should be evaluated by students as well as by each teacher and by the academic administration. One efficient and effective way to gain students' evaluations of their advising is to distribute an advising form (Exhibit 4.3) to every student on two different days each term—on days that will catch different class sequences. For example, the form can be submitted at 11:00 on Wednesday for the Monday-Wednesday-Friday class sequence and at another time, say 11:00 Thursday, to catch the Tuesday-Thursday class sequence. The same logic would apply to distributing the form for evening students who are an important group to have their advising views known.

DEVELOPING A FACULTY EVALUATION SYSTEM

Little has been written on steps in the process of developing a faculty evaluation system. This section outlines a systems approach that was developed by Bellevue Community College, Bellevue, Washington. See Appendix G for a very detailed, step-by-step description of how to develop this system.

1. Establish the committee.
2. Prepare the committee.

Exhibit 4.3
Student Evaluation of Instructor Advising

Name of Advisor ————————————————— Date ———————————

This form is designed to learn about how you evaluate the assistance and expertise of your advisor. The space at the end of the survey allows you to use your own words, and extra questions may be added if you wish. Your written comments will be summarized and typed so the instructor will not see your handwriting. Please do not sign your name.

The appraisal instrument is divided into two sections: (A) Academic Advising and (B) General Advising.

Directions: At the top of this form, please write the name of your assigned faculty advisor or counselor and also the date when you completed this form.

Each statement describes a basic component of advising. Evaluate your advisor on each item, giving the highest scores for very good performances and the lowest scores for very poor performances. Place in the blank space before each statement the number that most nearly expresses your evaluation on that item:

Highest			Middle			Lowest		No Opinion
7	6	5	4	3	2	1		X

A. *Academic Advising*

_____ 1. Keeps up-to-date on college regulations and course offerings.

_____ 2. Keeps office hours.

_____ 3. Keeps appointments when made in advance.

_____ 4. Plans for my academic programs are consistent with my academic objectives.

_____ 5. Maintains accurate files on my performance.

_____ 6. Advises in terms of course and program alternatives and encourages me to assume responsibility for these decisions.

_____ 7. Advises me effectively in my major areas of study.

_____ 8. Advises me on choices of courses that are meaningful to me but are not required.

B. *General Advising*

_____ 9. Is helpful to me in learning about the academic processes and procedures.

_____ 10. Listens to my points of view.

_____ 11. Is willing to use other college and/or community resources when my problems require views of others.

_____ 12. I am able to work toward solutions to my academic problems because of his/her advising assistance.

Exhibit 4.3 (*continued*)

_____ 13. I would return to this individual for assistance in the future.

_____ 14. _____

_____ 15. _____

_____ 16. Considering all of the items, this is my overall rating of his/her advising assistance.

Your written comments are welcome._____

_____

_____

_____

3. Assumptions regarding faculty evaluations should be clearly stated.

4. Define the purposes of faculty evaluations.

5. Determine specific objectives.

6. Determine the areas of faculty evaluation.

7. Establish the criteria for various areas chosen for faculty evaluation.

8. Develop instruments that will obtain needed information on the criteria.

9. Develop process and procedures for the faculty evaluation system.

10. Develop standards (achievement level) and weights for faculty evaluations.

11. Develop a grievance procedure.

12. Distribute proposed plan and obtain feedback.

13. Review all verbal and written feedback and make necessary changes.

14. Distribute revised proposal and obtain feedback.

15. Review feedback and prepare final document.

16. Distribute the final document.

17. Develop plan to review the evaluation system for the next few years.

18. Develop a plan to link faculty evaluation and faculty development.

19. Provide adequate professional preparation for personnel that will implement the evaluation process and procedures.

20. Don't get involved unless you are willing to put a considerable amount of time and effort into this endeavor.

CONCLUSION

Heisenberg (1967), one of the early leaders in theoretical atomic physics, developed the principle of indeterminacy, or the "uncertainty principle," which stated that the position and velocity of an electron cannot be measured simultaneously with high precision. The Heisenberg Principle is accepted by scientists as honest recognition of imprecision, yet it has not deterred the relentless pursuit of precision. Something of this spirit would seem appropriate to our pursuit of faculty evaluation. The data and procedures have their imprecisions, uncertainties, and threats, yet there is a vast amount of research, articles, expert opinions, and demands for better performances.

In the final analysis, only people can make systems, programs, or organizations work. The process of developing and implementing a system of faculty evaluation is a human problem. The sensitivities and fears of individuals are real and need always to be considered in developing and implementing any system, but progressive and dynamic two-year college programs and evaluations are developed and maintained by accentuating the positive and by moving ahead.

5

Focus on Improving

Organizations across the nation spend over $210 billion on formal and informal training and development for faculty members each year (U.S. Department of Education, 1993). For example, California community colleges spent $35.5 million, of which $4.9 million was from a special Faculty and Staff Development Fund established by the state legislature in 1988.

Three factors are relevant to this strong interest in professional development. The changing state and student demographics pose new challenges for higher education institutions. Faculty improvement programs can and should be designed to help faculty and staff improve their understanding of students from different ethnic, cultural, and social backgrounds. Many faculty members have been in their positions for twenty years or more and are in serious need of professional development and renewal. Also, very rapid expansion of computers and other technologies in education requires more or less continual updating in many fields.

A number of factors are promoting the growth and expansion of faculty development practices. The community college is a teaching institution where faculty are not expected to do university-type research, and they describe their colleges as "teach-or-perish" institutions. Indeed, the community college, in part, developed as a response to the preoccupation of universities with higher level professional knowledge and skills, although their development stems more directly from the needs of a robust national economy at the turn of the century that demanded many more workers with technical and/or entry-level skills.

Quality teaching does not result from good intentions. A characteristic that distinguishes college teaching from that done in secondary schools is that the college faculty seldom have had formal course work in pedagogy. People are hired to teach science because they appear to be exemplary scientists, and seldom are they required to demonstrate that they also are good teachers. Curricular design, the differences between testing for knowledge and testing for understanding, and techniques for challenging marginally motivated students are skill areas in which few two-year college faculty members have to demonstrate as a condition for being hired.

For technical programs, the teachers sometimes are hired more for their technical skills than their degrees, and they may not have had as many professional role models when they were students or else the idea of teaching someday may never have occurred to them. As a result, some two-year faculty members have not been "complete packages" when they assumed their teaching duties. Some faculty who have courses that require teaching both theory and practice are so uncomfortable in the lecturer's role that they mostly eliminate the lecture aspects in favor of demonstrations of how to perform the laboratory projects. In these instances students fail to get the theory and background information that provide the necessary context for the laboratory work to make sense. In one such class, a student who was in the middle of a laboratory project turned to her neighboring student and said, "I have no idea what I'm doing."

In the other extreme, some faculty bring such enthusiasm to their subject areas that they cannot stop talking about them, and the lectures significantly intrude into the prescribed laboratory time, thereby denying students the opportunity to develop their practical skills. This situation can be analogous to the father who buys an electric train for his child but will not stop showing him how to use it.

Still other kinds of problems can occur if faculty who are recruited from business, industry, or public service bring a mindset that is inappropriate for the classroom. One example is a former police officer who was hired to teach in a law enforcement technology course. An administrator visited his classroom and noted that the entire time was devoted to pure lecture. Later, the administrator asked the instructor if he ever considered allowing some class discussion. "No," came the reply, "I was hired to teach because I'm the expert. They are here because they don't know this material." As far as this instructor was concerned, the students by virtue of being students could not contribute much to the class.

People who are hired to teach but who are not prepared to do so can be very threatened by professional activities such as test item construction and course evaluation. One technical instructor who had worked in the industry most of his life simply refused to give low grades regardless of performance levels because he did not feel confident that students' low test scores were valid because he did not trust himself to write valid tests. In another incidence, a retired civil engineer in his first year of teaching was assigned a freshman physics course. Two weeks into the quarter he called the administrator who had hired him. "What do you want me to do now?" he asked. "I've covered the whole course and I have over three quarters of the term left." The administrator asked him, "Have you given them a test yet?" "No," admitted the instructor. "Well, give them a test over the material and let me know how they do." Two days later, the instructor called back to report, "I'm starting all over again; they didn't learn anything." These two anecdotes underscore the need for effective programs for faculty development.

Every community and technical college has several kinds of staff development activities but formidable and/or unfavorable forces can nullify some benefits. Improvement programs can take a negative, almost remedial, connotation and thereby evoke open or subtle resistance from otherwise receptive staff members. This is particularly true when teachers already believe their classroom performances are exemplary. Equally important are successes or failures of earlier staff improvement campus projects. A legacy or skeletons of earlier, ill-conceived staff improvement efforts can hinder solutions to perplexing campus problems such as declining enrollments, student retention, new instructional goals, and the introduction of new technologies. "The past is prologue" and past mistakes need to be acknowledged to clear the deck for new developments.

Developmental efforts also can be negatively affected by the belief that they are expensive and not very effective. Much growth in development programs during the 1970s can be attributed to receiving grant monies for faculty development, but when the external funding ended so did many of the programs. Several states have made special allocations for community college faculty development activities, although recent budget shortfalls have eliminated or significantly reduced some of them.

The cost and the effectiveness of faculty (staff) development activities are of genuine concern to two-year college administrators given the recent fiscal constraints in higher education. Developmental costs appear in most institutional budgets as activities such as conferences, tuition reimbursement, tuition waivers, teaching excellence awards, presidents' discretionary funds, instructional equipment and supplies, computer software, leaves with salary (sabbaticals), and professional books. Consolidation of departmental budget items under the heading of faculty improvement is in the best interests of institution-wide reforms, but possible political advantages of dispersing or "hiding" some of these activities also are a possibility.

Teaching improvement programs sometimes are an assembly of unrelated means in search of meaningful ends. Workshops, retreats, conferences, sabbaticals, consultations, in-service programs, graduate study, meetings of professional associations, faculty exchange programs, and professional libraries are examples of potentially valuable faculty development opportunities, but to what purpose? Linquist's 1978 statement is still relevant, noting that the programs to improve college teaching have three general purposes: "To effectively meet the learning needs of each student; to assist in the personal and professional development of each faculty member; and to promote the continuous development of institutional conditions which encourage and reward teaching improvement" (p. 253).

Too many professional development programs appear designed to self-destruct or to just fade away, and some colleges operate on the premise that anything is better than nothing. As a result they go with the lowest bidder for services and either hire presenters who are inadequate or overuse in-house presenters. In one instance a two-year college conducted an in-service session on total quality management in which the presenter stressed the need for flexibility, but that individual was known to be one of the most rigid persons in the college.

Staff support toward in-service programs can be lowered if programs are selected that have little or no bearing on the performance of their jobs or fail to address prominent campus issues. In one two-year college the administration surveyed the faculty and staff to learn how the college could be improved, only to learn that the overwhelming response was that performances at middle and first-line management levels were inadequate. In response to this feedback, the college contracted with a firm to offer dozens of workshops on various topics such as motivating others, time management, and communication. Instead of focusing on weaknesses among managers, the administration mandated that all employees attend a prescribed number of these presentations, which did little to address the findings of the survey. This response resulted in damaging the administration's credibility with rank-and-file employees.

Another administrative miscalculation might be to allow professional development activities to contradict the teaching mission of the college. For example, faculty members have been asked to attend off-campus workshops, conventions, or seminars, which requires the cancellation of classes. When it is judged that one or more faculty members should attend an off-campus event, administrators need to demonstrate a consistent valuing of student class time by giving faculty enough lead time to cover their classes with other instructors, videotape their lectures in advance, schedule guest speakers, or otherwise ensure that their students' education is not jeopardized in the pursuit of professional development. Failure to take these precautions can send the message that the value of quality teaching is situational.

Suitable programs and techniques of staff development do exist and can be adapted to the needs of campuses committed to maintaining vibrant faculties. Declining fiscal resources have forced instructional administrators to implement programs that encourage faculty growth and achievement in cost-effective ways.

FACULTY DEVELOPMENT STUDY

The Hopple study (1991) explored the extent, nature, and effectiveness of professional faculty development improvement practices in two-year institutions. This extensive national study described how development programs were organized, funded, and evaluated, and the extent to which faculty members participated in an array of development programs and activities. Included were 449 two-year community and technical colleges, which was approximately 40 percent of the national population, with a usable return rate of 70 percent. The Hopple study replicated one that was completed in 1976 by Centra for Educational Testing Services (ETS).

The thirty-four questionnaire items were designed to gain the information about developmental practices in the five areas of individual assistance, group-oriented institutional activities, institutional practices, and personal growth opportunities (see Exhibit 5.1).

The data will be presented in these five general areas, with subareas: systematic use of student ratings for improvement; faculty involvement in development activities; organizational structures for development and funding; evaluation of faculty development programs; and evaluation of development activities based on performance evaluation results.

Systematic Use of Student Ratings for Improvement

Both community and technical college administrators in Hopple's study gave very high ratings to systematic ratings of instruction by students and administrators for the purposes of improvement (Exhibit 5.1). The community college CAOs rated as very effective the use of master teachers, systematic ratings of instruction by students, and faculty with expertise consulting with other faculty on teaching or course improvement. Technical college leaders rated as most effective, in order of importance, using master teachers, a professional or personal development plan (growth contract), and systematic ratings of instructions by students. The least used of developmental practices given by both community and technical colleges was classroom visitation by de-

Exhibit 5.1
The Extent to Which 23 Development Practices Are Used in 50 Percent or More of 281 Community and Technical Colleges and Their Overall Ratings

	Ratings Within Categories	Overall Ratings
Individual Assistance Practices		
1. Specialists to help faculty develop teaching such as lecturing or leading discussions, or to encourage use of different teaching-learning strategies such as individualized instruction.	72	1
2. Specialists to assist faculty in constructing tests or evaluating student performance.	67	3
3. Specialists to assist individual faculty in instructional or course development by consulting course objectives and course design.	62	5
4. Simulated procedures which enable faculty to learn and practice specific teaching skills (e.g., microteaching.)	52	10
5. Assistance to faculty in use of instructional technology as a teaching aid (e.g., programmed learning or computer assisted instruction).	51	11
6. Classroom visitation by an instructional resource person (e.g., a developmental specialist), upon request, followed by a diagnosis of teaching.	50	12
Group-oriented Institutional Activities		
1. Workshops, seminars, or short courses that review subject matter or introduce new knowledge in a field.	68	2
2. Workshops or seminars on testing and evaluating student performance.	68	2
3. Workshops or programs in faculty effective development—improving their interpersonal skills or their ability to work effectively in groups, exploring educational values.	63	4
4. Workshops or presentations that explore general issues or trends in education.	60	6
5. Workshops or seminars dealing with new or different approaches to develop new curricula.	52	10

Exhibit 5.1 (*continued*)

6. Workshops or presentations that explore various methods or techniques of instruction.	50	12
7. Workshops, seminars, or programs to acquaint faculty with goals of the institution and types of students enrolled.	48	13

Institutional Practices

1. Use of grants by faculty members for developing new or different approaches to courses or teaching.	57	7
2. Sabbatical leaves with at least one-half salary.	56	8
3. A policy of unpaid leaves that covers educational or development purposes.	56	8
4. Summer grants for projects to improve instruction or courses.	50	12
5. Faculty exchange programs with other institutions.	48	13
6. Travel grants to refresh or update knowledge in a particular field.	48	13
7. There is a campus committee on faculty development.	45	14

Personal Growth Opportunities

1. Personal counseling provided to individual faculty members on career goals and other personal development areas.	54	9
2. Professional and personal development plan (sometimes called a growth contract) for individual faculty members.	50	12
3. Systematic ratings of instruction by students used to help faculty members.	43	14

Source: Hopple, 1991.

velopment specialists, although it was rated as over 50 percent effective.

The questionnaire included seven practices that involved the use of specialists to provide teaching assistance for faculty members. Audiovisual specialists were rated very effective to effective by over two-thirds of the respondents. Community college respondents reported that assistance to faculty and the uses of instructional technology attracted high faculty participation rates and were rated as 66 percent effective.

Specialists to assist faculty in student evaluation, instructional or course development, and teaching learning strategies or simulations that would enable faculty to learn and practice specific teaching skills were reported in less than one-third of the community colleges, but these institutions give them high effectiveness ratings. Special professional libraries devoted to teaching improvement were common and attracted a high percentage of faculty participation, but they were rated as the least effective of the assistance practices.

Two practices were used extensively in community colleges and were rated as highly effective. One practice, faculty visitations to other institutions or to other parts of their institution to review innovative projects, was used at 95 percent of the institutions and was considered effective or very effective by 73 percent of the colleges. Also, the practice of providing grants to faculty members for developing new or different approaches to teaching was used in 82 percent of the institutions and was considered effective or very effective at 73 percent of them. Faculty exchange programs and personal counseling of individual faculty members on career goals were used by less than one-third of the faculty at community colleges, but technical colleges said that they used this latter practice somewhat more extensively and found it to be 55 percent effective.

Items of Prominence

Of the thirty-four items included in this questionnaire, the use of travel funds to attend professional conferences was ranked as number four in usage and number one in effectiveness. Developmental use of student evaluations was ranked number two in usage and number eight in effectiveness.

The least effective practice was found to be the circulation of a development newsletter or other teaching-related material although it was used in over 77 percent of the reporting institutions.

The practice of allowing first-year faculty to have a lighter-than-normal teaching load was found at only 9 percent of the sample, although it was rated as 60 percent effective.

Faculty Involvement in Development Activities

In 25 percent of the community colleges, approximately 50 percent of the tenured and nontenured faculty were involved in various development activities according to Hopple's study. He found that respondents at 83 percent of the community colleges reported that 50 percent or more of their good teachers were involved in developmental programs, but in 55 percent of these colleges only 50 percent of the younger and less experienced teachers were even moderately involved in development activities. The most active group of participants were good teachers who wanted to be better.

Faculty members with over fifteen years of teaching experience were as active in participating in developmental activities as faculty members without continuing contracts. In 84 percent of community colleges the faculty members who really *needed* to improve were only minimally involved in development activities. Those who needed improvement the most want it the least.

Sixty-three percent of the technical colleges reported that 50 percent or more of their faculty members were involved in development activities, which is a higher percentage of faculty than reported by community colleges. Over 50 percent of the technical colleges said that the majority of their faculty in their first years of teaching participated in development activities, but they also reported that 66 percent of the faculty who needed to improve were only minimally involved in development programs. This finding is consistent with what Centra found in his 1976 study. Because participation in most development activities is voluntary, it is not surprising that good teachers comprise the major portion of participants. Because they are the most interested in teaching, they also are an important group to involve in development activities so that the program does not become labeled as a program for deficient teachers.

Organizational Structures for Development and Funding

Forty-five percent of the community colleges and 34 percent of the technical colleges had established organizational units or specific persons to coordinate developmental activities. These data indicate a negative trend in comparison to the earlier studies. Centra's study (1976) found that just under 49 percent of two-year colleges had established organizational units or specific persons, and Smith (1980) reported that 53 percent of community colleges had established organizational units or specific persons responsible for development activities. Smith reported that faculty development was not viewed as a critical aspect of the college's operation, noting that the responsibility for administering the developmental programs was an add-on responsibility to those already held by line managers who may take less than an enthusiastic approach to the additional work load.

Median Age of Developmental Units

Hopple's study found that campus units had a median existence of three years while these units in technical colleges had a median age of five years. Centra (1976) reported the median age of two-year college development units was 2.5 years. Since these two studies were separated in time by fifteen years, the implication is that most of the current programs are either new to the institutions surveyed by Hopple or during this fifteen-year period they ceased to exist and have been resurrected in the last six to eight years.

Source of Internal Funding

Community colleges reported that an average of 66 percent of the total budget for developmental activities came from the institution's general fund, while technical colleges reported receiving 77 percent of their developmental funds from other sources. Grants from foundations and/or the federal government averaged 10 percent at community colleges and 6 percent at technical colleges. Community colleges reported that an additional 19 percent came from state funds while technical colleges reported 15 percent from this source. Community colleges reported that they received 4 percent of their fiscal support from other sources such as endowments or special purpose funds, and technical colleges acknowledged receiving 2 percent from these sources.

Percentage of Institutional Budget for Developmental Activities

Sixty-seven percent of community colleges allocated less than 1 percent of the total institutional budget for development appropriations, while 27 percent spent between 2 and 4 percent. The percentage of total institutional budget spent on faculty development at technical colleges was less than 4 percent, and 78 percent of them had an expenditure of 1 percent or less. The low level of funding and the finding that almost one-half of the community and technical colleges' development budgets have remained at the same levels of funding over the previous two years indicate that in view of problems with fiscal inflation and declining financial resources the two-year colleges had, in reality, declining developmental resources at the time of the Hopple study (1991). There is no compelling evidence that significant improvements have been made since then.

Evaluation of Faculty Developmental Programs

Twenty-four percent of the community colleges reported regular evaluation of their development programs, 37 percent reported partial evaluations, and another 37 percent indicated that they had not evaluated these programs. Nine percent of the technical colleges had evaluated their development programs, 40 percent performed partial evaluations, and 51 percent had not conducted evaluations. Centra (1976) reported that 19 percent of the two-year colleges completed evaluations and another 35 percent had performed partial evaluations. Less than a 10 percent improvement in program evaluation was evident between 1976 and 1991.

Considering that over fifteen years elapsed between Centra's 1976 and Hopple's 1991 studies, very little gain had occurred in the area of evaluating development programs; there is little evidence or reason to believe much has changed since 1991. This evidence can be important in justifying and in increasing financial support and also for providing baseline data for changing or improving development programs. Much improvement is needed in this area.

Evaluation of Development Activities Based on Performance Evaluation Results

Both Zitlow's evaluation study (1988) and Hopple's development study indicated that about 50 percent of all two-year colleges regularly used performance, principally classroom teaching, evaluation information to provide direction in establishing their development activities for faculty members. Zitlow reported that of the 331 CAOs responding, just over 55 percent said that faculty evaluation results were used for planning and designing development programs. Institutions without faculty unions reported that about 64 percent utilized evaluation results in the design of faculty development programs and activities, and a slightly smaller percentage of smaller colleges with enrollments of less than 4,000 students (59 percent) reported that they used faculty evaluation data for developmental evaluation.

Two years later when Hopple asked essentially the same general question, just under 50 percent of reporting institutions said that faculty performance evaluation information was used as input to the design of faculty development activities. Again, the smaller colleges reported using evaluation data somewhat more frequently than did the larger institutions but less than in the earlier evaluation study by Centra. This downward trend raises some questions concerning not only the effectiveness but also the longevity of faculty development programs at institutions where the results of faculty evaluation and faculty development are viewed as two separate and distinct activities.

CONCLUSION

Both instructors and administrators require systematic and sustained professional efforts just to keep abreast in most fields and occupations, and even greater efforts to stay "ahead of the curve." Community colleges' primary source of pride is their focus on providing excellent teaching, and to allow this focus to erode would deprive two-year schools of their greatest service to students and best selling points. Technical and community colleges also survive by being able to offer excellent programs that are current or ahead of developments in their fields. In the new technologies as well as in some more traditional occupations, faculty evaluation and development are essential parts of upgrading attitudes and skills. This reality places heavy burdens upon budgets to provide faculty teaching enrichment opportunities on a regular basis, and it places additional professional responsibilities on individuals to be creative in finding professional renewal opportunities where institutional fiscal resources are limited—which is quite often. And in terms of the individual teacher: When you're through learning, you're through!

6

Designing and Implementing
Professional Improvement Systems

Every community and technical college participates in various types of staff development activities, but the composite can look like a quilt—a number of pieces with little overall planning and modest coordination. An important decision to be made in revising or implementing staff and faculty improvement and evaluation programs relates to scope and coordination of instructional programming and its evaluation. Evaluation often is the forgotten or minor factor.

ORGANIZATIONAL PATTERNS AND MODELS

Some earlier faculty improvement programs were based upon the belief that in-service education was the responsibility of every program coordinator, with the general result that everybody's responsibility often became no one's responsibility. There is general agreement in the literature and in practice that successful programs are managed by at least one full-time faculty improvement person who reports to the institution's chief instructional officer. To assist the development coordinator an advisory committee of faculty members is generally used, sometimes including chairs and other administrators.

Prominent organizational location of staff improvement leadership provides these services with some institutional leverage, visibility, and a direct relationship to academic units and other services that are needed to obtain human and material support for various programs. A staff rather than line responsibility largely frees this activity from the threat of excessive supervision and personnel decision making while providing flexibility in defining and implementing its functions.

The model programs that have been used in two-year colleges include the National Institute for Staff and Organizational Development (NISOD) model for professional development; teaching improvement process (TIP) model; an in-service educational model; the "institutionalized" staff development model; and the staff development committee approach. An inventory of the characteristics that promote faculty growth and instructional change through these five models should be studied in developing a comprehensive model that incorporates the means for administering the programs, activities that could be used to promote professional improvement, resources for funding the programs, and a plan for evaluating the program.

Hopple found that 45 percent of the 281 reporting community colleges and 34 percent of the 156 reporting technical colleges said that they had a unit or person who coordinated developmental activities. These units are typically managed by a staff development coordinator or director, or a development committee, and report to the chief instructional officer. As would be expected, medium and large community colleges have a larger number of people involved in developmental activities. One-third of the larger colleges belong to consortia or regional groups that focus on faculty development. Consortia arrangements can be helpful in securing greater audiences and greater human and material support for workshops and seminars.

A MODEL FOR INSTITUTION-WIDE EVALUATION OF A FACULTY IMPROVEMENT PROGRAM

Every college needs an institutional model for improving and evaluating the college's developmental program, and the model should be communicated within the institution. Such a model can serve to enhance the support for developmental activities and to provide some concrete evidence of the connectedness of the various developmental programs.

Annual evaluations of developmental programs should be undertaken in a manner that allows comparisons over time, and the college's faculty development committee is the logical group to undertake this annual process, perhaps augmented by an individual from the institutional research office and another person representing the office of the chief instructional officer. Exhibit 6.1 is a comprehensive improvement model with brief explanatory notes following in each sector.

1. Basic Assumptions

A. Everyone can, and should, improve. While the pace and nature of improvement will vary greatly, it is the institution's responsibility to provide ample opportunities and meaningful incentives to enhance improvement.

B. Professional growth opportunities should be individualized. Fulfilling this assumption is much easier said than done; nevertheless if it is internalized and some resources committed, more individualized improvement will take place.

C. Professional opportunities should be diversified. Professional development programs should seek to diversify opportunities as much as quality and costs will allow, but there are some risks in too much diversity whereby limited resources are spread so widely that the impact of individual programs can suffer. Diversity requires practical creativity—practical in that expensive programs for few needs must be weighed against less expensive programs for many. In some cases when institutional mission and/or programmatic thrusts are considered, the more expensive programs for a relatively few individuals may be chosen. Institutional missions and programmatic considerations should be carefully weighed.

D. Professional opportunities should improve teaching performance. Progress toward fulfilling this assumption depends not only on being committed to it but also on committing optimal human and material resources to programs. Also, ways and means for evaluating programs and activities need to be developed. They can include personal statements about improvements and successes, statements from colleagues and from administrators who work closely with the developmental activities, from outside consultants, and from student evaluations of the programs. And shortcomings should be aired and considered as means toward improved ends.

2. Operational Principles

A. Optimal institutional human and material resources are necessary,

Exhibit 6.1

A Conceptual Framework for Developing, Managing, and Evaluating a Faculty Development Program

BASIC COMPONENTS

	Teaching Improvement			Course Improvement			Professional Updating			Personal Development			Institutional Renewal	
Qualitative judgments about value/effectiveness of each basic component using these criteria	Workshops/institutes	Campus faculty improvement programs	Campus/fiscal assistance	Technological aids	Course modifications	Campus fiscal assistance	Sabbatical leave	Short-term leaves	Institutes/ workshops	Personal development	Campus fiscal assistance	Study of institutional-wide concerns	Preparation for new roles	Institutional responsibilities
Planning														
Doing(Managing and Doing)														
Evaluating														
Funding														
Organizing														
Communicating														

A numerical rating scale of 5 to 1 can be used for evaluating each applicable item and its sub-categories.

but successful programs have been developed "on a shoestring." Those who sit around waiting until satisfactory funds are forthcoming may have a long wait. Most success stories in higher education come from one person having an idea and not being deterred from those who say, "It will never fly." The world moves ahead on the backs of doers and so it is with faculty improvement programs. Years ago some South Sea Island natives had what is called a "cargo cult" mentality about their problems. They thought that some day a ship would come sailing into their bay loaded with precious gems and gold and their problems would be solved. Some advocates for faculty development programs have something of a similar attitude when they contend that generous human and material resources are necessary to develop a faculty development program. The following example happened in a moderately sized state public university in the northeast. In the mid-1970s, when faculty and staff reductions were mandated by fiscal shortfalls, a professor in psychology wanted to start a faculty development program. Without money and with one-half released time from teaching, he developed his first faculty development newsletter with the encouragement of the chief academic officer. This four-page, locally oriented newsletter found a title that provided a catalyst and perhaps an essential initial spark to what became a very respectable and useful university publication. The title was "FTE," standing not for the usual "full-time equivalent," but "For Teaching Excellence."

B. Development programs should be crafted around the most *basic* faculty needs *on the campus*. The data from the Hopple study can provide useful starting points and can serve as a checklist for the campus, but every campus should develop its own survey of faculty views on activities to enhance classroom learning. Such a survey can be repeated every two years or so as a check on how teaching and learning activities mesh with faculty perceptions of them. Appendix H gives the faculty excellence survey used successfully by Miami-Dade Community College.

C. The program should build upon modest successes moving toward greater ones. The program and all changes and additions should be planned carefully. Crash programs usually crash, yet time is not always on the side of gradualism.

3. Basic components. The conceptual framework in Exhibit 6.1 has five basic components: (A) teaching improvement, (B) course improvement, (C) professional updating, (D) personal development, and (E) institutional renewal. Examples are given in each of these components, but institutions need to consider including their own components.

A. *Teaching improvement* includes the range of developmental activities that are listed in Hopple's study plus others. The conceptual model lists workshops, institutes, faculty improvement programs, and campus financial assistance for activities such as attending workshops and special short courses.

B. *Course improvement* includes activities such as technological aids, course modifications, and campus fiscal assistance for items such as equipment and supplies, and attending targeted seminars and short courses.

C. *Professional updating* includes activities such as taking paid or unpaid leaves and other opportunities, attending institutes and workshops, and individualized study programs. This category is very important for all fields of study but particularly in the medically related sciences and technology fields. To keep up and stay on the cutting edge of most fields is a never-ending challenge—one that most all colleges recognize and support verbally but do not always support with optimal human and material resources.

D. *Personal development* includes broadening and deepening experiences that may be closely related to one's professional field or that may be quite different. For example, a young instructor may wish to move into community college administration and believes that attending a course or workshop in this area might help, or someone may wish to develop expertise in another professional area such as computer science.

E. *Institutional renewal* refers to a wide range of activities. One may wish to undertake a detailed study of a college's retention successes and failures, or another individual may wish to attend a workshop and purchase books to improve teaching. Also, upon assuming chair of the institution-wide appointment and continuing appointment committee, a faculty member may have a need for some fiscal support for additional extracurricular study time and attendance at a relevant workshop.

4. Judging Value/Effectiveness of Each Basic Component. Each basic component of the professional development model needs to be evaluated as to its efficiency and effectiveness as well as to its value to the individual, the unit, and/or the college.

This conceptual framework allows a college or a unit to view the institution as a whole as well as in terms of its component parts. This approach can use numerical value judgments, and there is value in having these data, but numbers alone do not tell the whole story. Therefore, supplementary and subjective data should be gathered to enrich numerical inputs.

Exhibit 6.2
Training and Development Matrix

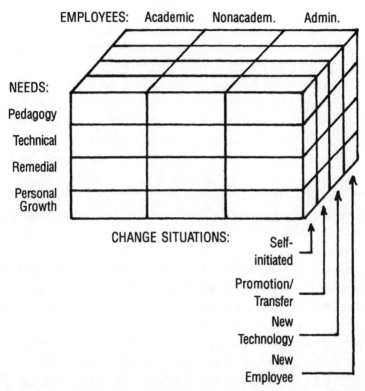

Source: Miller and Holzapfel, eds., *Issues in Personnel Management*, 1988.

A MATRIX MODEL FOR DEVELOPMENT

A matrix model for faculty development (Exhibit 6.2) was developed by Rostek and Kladivko and reported in Miller (1988). The model addresses the four developmental areas of pedagogical needs, technical needs, remedial needs, and personal growth. The employee axis is divided into academic, nonacademic, and administrative categories. The academic category includes faculty members whose major responsibility is classroom instruction; the nonacademic category includes clerical, maintenance, and other support personnel; and the administrative category primarily includes chairs and deans. The second axis represents the kinds of needs that staff development can address, which are pedagogical, technical/professional, remedial, and/or personal growth. The third axis gives four change situations: needs of newly hired employees, needs resulting from technological changes, needs caused by promotions and transfers, and needs related to self-initiated activities in each of the four need categories.

Staff development programs available to a college's personnel can be enhanced by the variables in the matrix. For example, activities useful for support staff may not be applicable to faculty; likewise, instruction in pedagogy would probably be of little benefit to clerical or maintenance personnel. The matrix includes forty-eight cells into which training and development activities can be placed, and the major developmental activities of each employee can be placed in any one of sixteen cells. It is important that a generic approach to development not overlook the varied needs of individuals.

Exhibit 6.3, for example, can be used for newly hired faculty members or for personnel hired directly from business and industry with little or no teaching experience. However, even teaching experience is no guarantee that one understands variations in learning styles, construction of tests and evaluation methods, curriculum development, and various methods of instruction.

Exhibit 6.4 can be useful for a chairperson who needs developmental work for the move from chairperson to dean, for example. This program could be technical and personal growth, nonacademic and administration, and related to at least two of the four change situations. In general, this matrix enables program developers to make better decisions about which types of developmental activities are needed for varied positions and individuals.

Faculty and staff members on continuing contract also can benefit from professional energization from outside of themselves. The chair and/or dean comes into the evaluation formula but hopefully with some evidence beyond hearsay. A self-appraisal form for professional growth evaluation can be helpful (see Exhibit 6.5) along with a narrative statement that is developed by each individual. The appropriate administrator can fill in the same standardized form as well as write a narrative statement

Exhibit 6.3
Training and Development Matrix: New Faculty Member Wanting
Pedagogical Skills

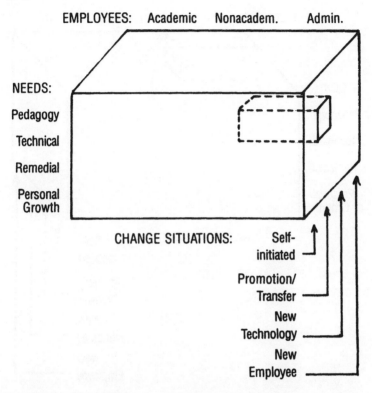

Source: Miller and Holzapfel, eds., *Issues in Personnel Management*, 1988.

where appropriate. The two forms can be discussed at the developmental conference between each faculty member and the chairperson.

Professional growth should be the outcome of professional development, but how can it be measured? The "calibrated eyeball" or the "attentive ear" are not sufficient although they do have a place. Appraisal or judgment of professional developmental growth should be done by the individual, by the chair and/or dean, and sometimes by a committee of peers. The last may be a paper tiger that is unrealistic for the very busy world of two-year college professionals unless the assignment is taken

Exhibit 6.4
Training and Development Matrix: Chairperson Wanting
Administrative Skills for Promotion to Dean

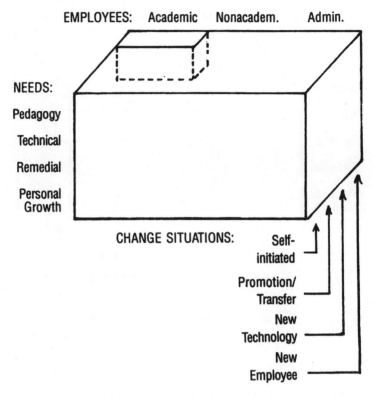

Source: Miller and Holzapfel, eds., *Issues in Personnel Management*, 1988.

seriously. Many colleges do have standing committees on staff personnel matters that could look into professional growth for those staff members who are pursuing continuous contracts (tenure). But how about the faculty members who are on permanent appointment?

CONCLUSION

Inadequate attention paid to the processes of change can be fatal. Good ideas do not implement themselves; people do. The best designed systems will flounder if implementation is left to chance. Failure-prone factors are worthy of consideration al-

Exhibit 6.5
Professional Growth Evaluation

Name of Teacher ————————————— Academic Year ————

Appraiser ——————————————— Title ———————————

Professional growth comprises those professional activities that can assist one in keeping a sense of scholarship, learning, teaching improvement, optimism, and future orientation. It interrelates to teaching, scholarship, and cutting edge materials and thinking.

Directions: Please rate the individual on each item, giving the highest scores for exceptional performances and the lowest scores for very poor performances. Additional questions may be added as items 6 and 7.

Highest			Middle			Lowest		Don't Know
7	6	5	4	3	2	1		X

_____ 1. Attends campus-based programs that are relevant to knowledge or pedagogical advancement (professional renewal).

_____ 2. Attends campus-based or off-campus programs that can assist in professional renewal.

_____ 3. Keeps up to date in his/her professional field through membership in appropriate organizations and societies as well as in other ways such as workshops and reading.

_____ 4. Seeks professional improvement by developing and using innovative and/or new programs and activities in the classroom or laboratory.

_____ 5. Expresses interest in renewal and is innovative.

_____ 6. ——————————————————————————————

_____ 7. ——————————————————————————————

_____ 8. Considering all of the items, this is the overall rating of professional growth.

Comments:

——————————————————————————————————————

——————————————————————————————————————

——————————————————————————————————————

though we rarely admit failure in higher education, nor do we usually examine our mistakes constructively. Agriculturists analyze crop failures; doctors perform autopsies; in higher education, we write another proposal! Failure-prone strategies include:

- weak, clandestine, or indecisive project leadership;
- insensitivity of overenthusiastic advocates;
- nominal or token support at the top;
- poor timing in terms of campus or complications of communication;
- poorly designed plans or excessively complex plans; and
- failure to realize the human propensity not to change.

Resistance to change is age-old, as Francis Bacon noted in 1597 in his *On Innovation*: "It is true that what is settled by custom, though it be not good, at least it is fit. And those things which have long gone together are as it were confederate within themselves; whereas new things piece not so well; but though they help by their utility, yet they trouble by their unconformity. Besides, they are like strangers, more admired and less favored."

7

Making Faculty Personnel Decisions

A college is three things—people, programs, and places—and in that order of importance. Therefore, decision making about the instructional staff is the most important activity undertaken by a college.

HIRING

In athletics what happens on the playing field will be determined significantly by the quality of recruiting. So is the case with recruiting new full-time and adjunct faculty members in two-year and four-year colleges. Some of the most common recruiting methods include the use of printed job opportunity advertising, word-of-mouth, and employment agencies. However, just as successful athletic coaches carefully plan their recruiting strategy, so do successful community and technical colleges. Each method of recruiting needs forethought and planning for best professional results as well as for optimal liability avoidance.

Watts (1993, p. 30) noted that "the most successful searches are those that consider the selection as a process and proceed through a well-defined set of activities." In a search process model, he suggested the following series of steps that "proceed from pre-search to search to post-search activities."

1. Pre-search: The pre-search involves appointing a search committee and preparing the advertisement for the position. Also included in

this step is the careful screening of applicants on paper, including a search of references as well as a screening interview if practical.

2. Search: The search committee at this stage would conduct the interviews from the narrowed applicant pool and would conclude the investigation with the selection.

3. Post-search: The post-search involves the making of the offer of employment and following up to make his or her transition to the institution as smooth as possible. It is this final step, the transition to the institution, that can mean a dedicated staff member or another search due to attrition later.

Full-Time Staff Members

Many two-year colleges do not pay enough attention to recruiting and selecting instructional personnel, perhaps a nostalgic carryover from times when the pace and scope of academe were slower and more casual, and possibly it is a result of the frantic 1960s when "warm bodies" were sought to fill personnel needs created by the building boom. Whatever the causes, the search processes reflect the reality that colleges create their future through their hiring practices.

The search processes for full-time instructors can have five distinct yet related aspects: selecting the search committee, advertising the position, interviewing the final pool, selecting the prime candidate, and concluding negotiations. Also to be considered in the hiring of new staff members is the equitable evaluation of each applicant. "Consistency in the evaluation of candidates is essential to standards of fairness. Committee members who use measurable criteria for all candidates have a clearer view of each individual" (Lawhon and Ennis, 1995, p. 353).

It might be added that the more that is known about the candidates, the more successful decisions will be. To this end, many departments go beyond traditional resumes and interviews by inviting the most qualified candidate to present a lesson or paper to the full-time faculty. More than one department has been saved from making a poor choice by observing the candidate's teaching performance.

Adjunct Staff Members

The circumstances of part-time instructors were clearly stated by Roueche, Roueche, and Milliron (1996, p. 34):

Perhaps the greatest irony . . . is that part-timers represent the largest faculty cohort in American community colleges. Currently, the total number of part-time faculty is twice that of full-time faculty. Moreover, the total hours and the curriculum areas that they most frequently teach put them squarely in the face of the most challenging missions of the community college—the instruction of under prepared and at risk students. . . . Given these dynamics—the interplay between standard treatment, sheer numbers, important roles, and actual benefits to the institution—it is especially curious that part-time faculty can still be justifiably described as "strangers in their own land."

The search processes for adjunct or part-time instructors should be checked to see if they are systematic, comprehensive, and professional. Ways of hiring through conversations such as, "Do you know anyone who can teach?" are highly suspect, yet informal channels can be very useful. More formal approaches are preferred, however. In any case it is important to have thoroughly spelled-out processes for selecting adjunct faculty. As Erwin and Andrews (1993, p. 557) noted, "Minimum qualifications act as a guide to lure qualified candidates. More than one institution has had its casual adjunct hiring practices come back to haunt them through law suits, negative newspaper stories, and/or student withdrawals."

Financial stringencies have forced many two-year colleges to look more carefully at filling each position as well as at whether the vacancy can be put to better use in another unit. Avakian (1995, p. 35) noted that "the adjunct faculty member track has been perceived by institutions as a quick fix to offering more teaching for less money. Since fringe benefits are not offered to adjunct faculty members, institutions have more latitude to cope with budgetary swings of legislative appropriations." Such institution-wide considerations suggest that colleges should have a resource allocation model that can be used to compare the human and material teaching resources of various instructional units.

Mission and scope compatibility is another important perspective that is used in ascertaining the unit's present and future needs. It requires a strong data base, over time, which in turn requires a solid institutional research capability within the institution.

Restructuring of traditional academic careers will continue into the future, and it will include more females and minorities, more part-time and noncontinuing appointments, and restricted teacher mobility. A college teaching position a few years ago was a place to hang one's hat, but now it is a place to hang on to.

MINORITY HIRING AND RETENTION

Community and technical colleges are multicultural institutions of higher education with diverse students, faculty, and staffs. More than 25 percent of the total community and technical college student body is comprised of people of color. Piland and Silva (1996, p. iii) noted that by the year 2020, demographers predict that minorities will compose nearly one-third of the country's population and nearly one-half of the school-age youth.

Carter (1994, p. 15) wrote that the employment of two-year faculty of color only partially mirrors the four-year sector. "Unlike four-year colleges and university campuses, where faculty of color hold tenure at lower than average rates, in two-year colleges African American, American Indian, Hispanic American, and Asian American full-time faculty hold tenured positions at rates slightly above the national average."

But the national picture of the ethnic composition of two-year colleges' board members does not reflect the racial background of their student bodies. According to Vaughan and Weisman (1997), the recent national ethnic composition is 86.6 percent Caucasian; 7.9 percent African-American; 2.3 percent Hispanic; 1.1 percent Asian-American; 0.8 percent Native American; and 1.2 percent "other." Also, faculty of color do not fare as well as white faculty in achieving senior academic rank, and a much larger share of minority faculty are at lecturer and instructor levels.

Inflexibility of some current permanent appointment/tenure systems has contributed to the problems in higher education. Magner (1995, pp. A17–18) noted that "if there are going to be limited opportunities, how are we going to accommodate minorities?" The accommodation of minorities is one of the problems of the current tenure system. This is because "there hasn't been any real growth in the proportion of tenured faculty. The tenured quota system has contributed to that."

Many community colleges are giving greater attention to persons of color when evaluating the applicant pool as well as greater attention to the disabled. The Americans with Disabilities Act (ADA) "provides protection for approximately 43 million Americans or about one out of six" (Lawhon and Ennis, 1995, p. 356); therefore, some changes in recruiting and hiring, such as changing the physical requirements of a job, may be necessary to meet the standards established by the ADA.

IMPROVING

Every year each full-time instructional staff member should have two formal meetings with the chair, dean, or some other designated institutional official. One conference is the Annual Developmental Review (ADR), and the other is the Annual Performance Review (APR). One might ask "Why not combine them and save everyone's time?" While related, both are distinct in their own right and each is important. Are two annual meetings about the main business of the college—improving and judging teaching—too much time to spend? If "people" are the most important resource of a college, then time will be found. McGee (1995, p. 344) noted that "the typical interval between evaluations was one year for non-tenured personnel and three years for tenured faculty." What currently is typical is not adequate.

Annual Developmental Review

An Annual Developmental Review (ADR) is scheduled by each chair for each instructional staff member in the unit during every academic year. It allows the chairperson, the head, or designated administrator to have at least one serious, structured, and documented conversation each year about the main business of the college—teaching and including other matters as well.

Each session can focus upon a common core set of questions in addition to special ones that the chair or individual staff member wants to include. The core set of questions can include:

1. What are the special aspects of your instructional assignments since the last conference?
2. What are your noteworthy teaching and nonteaching accomplishments?
3. What problems and/or difficulties have you encountered during the past year?
4. What new or different professional activities would you like to try in the future?
5. What can *we* do to improve the operations and atmosphere of the unit?

This process is suggested: The time and place of the forty-five-minute to one-hour meeting are confirmed by a brief memo. The meeting should not be rushed, and the scheduling of the various meetings should be over a sufficiently longer period of time so the chair's office does not become a revolving door of ADR meetings. The chair writes a summary of each meeting, sending the individual a copy as well as including a copy in the individual's personnel file. The individual faculty member knows that he or she can write a rejoinder for the files and/or schedule another meeting.

JUDGING

What are the purposes of the promotion and continuing appointment (tenure) processes? Some colleges have not given adequate attention to these basic purposes while acknowledging the crucial importance of these decisions to the quality and growth of the institution. The following purposes are some suggested guidelines.

• *Academic promotion and continuing appointment policies and procedures help assure that students have sound teaching and learning opportunities by providing competent and current teachers.* This statement places students at the center of the educational process. Many two-year colleges have dramatically improved their student services over the past decade, but "the golden age of the student," as outlined in Clark Ken's book for the Carnegie Council on Policy Studies in Higher Education, *Three Thousand Futures* (1980, p. 53), has not yet come to pass. This first purpose places students' learning first among organizational goals, not just in words but in deeds.

• *The promotion and continuing appointment processes can provide an important developmental period for new faculty members.* Sometimes the "settled" faculty and administrators forget about their first few hectic years of teaching. A new instructor moves into a new community and becomes immersed immediately in a new professional environment. The need is to "hit the ground running" and to learn as quickly as possible the folkways, history, procedures, prominent people, expectations, and those new courses and preparations. To complicate matters further, newcomers may be assigned some of the largest classes at the least desirable times. And of course there are other "minor" things such as buying and selling residences, schools, shopping, and always added costs. During these early times the new faculty member is scrutinized, usually obliquely, but nonetheless intensely, by senior staff members and administrators. The unfortunate part of this scrutiny may be the lack of direct and systematic professional feedback along the way—a lack of communication that could leave the institution vulnerable to legal action at a later time.

• *Continuing appointment decisions should strengthen the instructional component of the college.* In the final analysis, colleges move ahead or fall behind based upon the quality of their instructional programs. Each new appointment and continuing appointment decision should serve as a building block toward enhancing instructional excellence.

CHARACTERISTICS OF EFFECTIVE PROMOTION AND APPOINTMENT DECISIONS

A number of characteristics of effective promotion and tenure systems can be identified, not so much from the sparse research evidence on this important matter as from instructional administrators' experiences. McCabe and Jenrette (1993, p. 25) noted that "an institution is truly supporting teaching and learning when policies and practices (1) select faculty on the basis of teaching skills and interests, (2) orient and help new faculty understand their institutional duties, (3) help faculty build teaching skills throughout their careers, (4) hold individuals accountable for performance, and (5) recognize and reward valued performance areas of faculty evaluation." (See Appendix B for a statement of "Teaching/Learning Values at Miami-Dade Community College.")

The Academic Promotion and Appointment Policies and Procedures Should Reflect the History and Nature of the Institution

All colleges have their own traditions that significantly affect promotion and appointment decisions, sometimes in ways not known even to some senior faculty members who often believe, and not without some reason, that they are the conscience and heart of the institution.

Institutional traditions may change rapidly as a result of external influences such as changes in leadership, although usually internal change is fairly slow, as Hefferlin (1969, p. 24) noted: "During normal times . . . the major process of academic change is that of accretion and attrition: the slow addition and subtraction of functions to existing structures." Developing promotion and appointment criteria that are appropriate to the institution is much easier said than done, yet sustained efforts can reduce the chances of awkward mismatches.

The System Is Compatible with Current Institutional Goals and Objectives

Goals are the larger purposes and long-range plans for the whole institution. They may be barely measurable but nonetheless they provide important overall directions. Objectives are short-range targets that usually can be achieved in one to five years. As a rule of thumb, collegiate institutions should plan "hard" for five years and "soft" for ten years.

It is important that senior institutional management has overall control of the nature and direction of promotion and tenure decisions. For example, instructors in fields of study that are growing and in the mainstream of the institution's overall development might be more likely to receive faster advancement than those in instructional fields that are shrinking. This marketplace concept continues to receive strong criticism from those in the humanities and the fine arts. A teacher of English has every reason to believe that his or her chosen life's work is as important as computer science; indeed, some colleges have developed academic reward systems based on equity among fields of study. On the other hand, our technologically oriented nation is striving to remain internationally competitive, which means that chief executives and chief instructional officers, sometimes under pressure from governing boards, must vie with other institutions for talented professionals in some technological fields. This dilemma is likely to become more pronounced in the years ahead.

Advancement policies and procedures at the institutional, divisional, and departmental levels should be consistent. Some new presidents find that 80 percent of the faculty members are tenured, and in some units the figure is closer to 100 percent. This reality can create difficulties for CEOs and CAOs who are personally motivated or instructed by governing boards to increase academic program flexibility or to reduce costs by reducing staff.

The College Needs to Balance Its Instructional Needs with the Individual's Professional Interests

This challenge is an ever present one, and the balance changes from time to time with changing external conditions and institutional priorities. Braskamp and Ory (1994, pp. 21–22) addressed the dilemma in this manner:

faculty assessment must incorporate the individual and the institutional perspectives. Focusing on one perspective only produces an incomplete assessment. The paradox of simultaneously giving faculty their independence and providing some type of monitoring will never be fully resolved, only acknowledged and confronted. Helping others develop means assessing and giving feedback, which requires a caring attitude.

This question of institutional priorities also was discussed earlier by Scriven (1978, p. 1) who wrote about the "value" and "merit" dimensions of evaluation. The "worth" of the individual to the institution is primarily an institutional-level decision, whereas the "merit" of the individual is primarily a professional judgment based upon academic credentials and performance and is determined primarily by professional colleagues. A tilt toward merit is usually evident in promotion decisions; worth considerations become more important in continuing appointment decisions. In practice, something of this differentiation does take place, although making decisions about worth and merit often are far from being clear cut.

The System Encompasses Both Institutional and Departmental Expectations

The institutional perspective encompasses administrative, legal, and humane considerations. Administrative considerations include the official faculty handbook's statements about promotion and tenure as well as statements issued by the CAO. Institutional positions should be compatible with departmental criteria, and relevant institution-wide statements should be appended to departmental statements. Sometimes even little differences among the various institutional statements can be significant. For example, a unit in one college asked applicants for promotion or continuing appointment to list all professional activities for only the previous five years, while the procedures issued by the CAO asked appointment applicants to provide *curricula vitae* that listed all professional activities in their entire careers. Unless a department head incorporated the instructions about the chief academic officer's preference, an applicant's case might be weakened at the CAO level by the omission of a complete *curriculum vitae*.

Another problem can arise when the different institutional administrative levels fail to coordinate their respective personnel expectations. Most departments and colleges want to see detailed documentation, but the institution's academic office may prefer to see only a covering summary notebook. A box or two of documentation sent to the institution's academic office when written instructions do not require or politely discourage it, will not be well received and may detract from an applicant's evaluation. Sometimes colleges have little or no written communication of expectations among the various levels of decision making. This shortcoming needs to be corrected.

The Appointment and Promotion Policies and Procedures Are Clearly Articulated in Written Documents

Most colleges have written policy statements, but many fewer also have established procedures for implementing and evaluating them.

The American Association of University Professors (AAUP) has had a consistent policy on fair procedures in dismissal cases since its first statement in 1915. In this classical statement by the Committee on Academic Freedom and Academic Tenure (AAUP, 1915, pp. 41–42), the policy stated the right of "every university or college teacher ... before dismissal or demotion, to have the charges against him stated in writing in specific terms and to have a fair trial on those charges before a special or permanent committee chosen by the faculty senate or council, or by the faculty at large." The AAUP issued similar statements in 1925, 1940, 1958, 1970, and 1982. Considering these and the general oral support in academe for written policies and procedures for judging promotion and permanent appointment, one wonders why detailed procedural statements are not more evident in two-year colleges. One reason may be that some colleges have not given adequate attention to academic personnel management policies and procedures, or a second reason may be the quiet preference of some governing boards and senior administrators to have very general policies and procedures for academic promotion and tenure because vagueness is thought to provide a greater degree of flexibility in making these decisions. However, in the present litigation-prone climate, colleges would be wise to have their personnel policies and procedures checked periodically by legal authorities that specialize in higher education.

The Policies and Procedures Are Applied Consistently and Fairly

Little research has focused on the satisfactions and dissatisfactions of faculties, administrators, and governing boards with the processes of administering and evaluating promotion and continuing appointment cases. If faculty members feel "an aura of mystery" about the promotion and tenure processes, they may conclude that these policies and procedures are not applied consistently or fairly. The significant number of court cases on these matters also should be considered. Processes should be consistent, clearly stated, and applied equitably to all faculty members. In addition, one should ask whether the personnel policies and procedures in departments are appropriate to the quality and expectations of the department as well as those of the institution. It can be difficult for colleges to blend realism with optimism when considering appraisal criteria in relation to market realities and institutional aspirations. But these problems and dilemmas need to be addressed openly.

The Overall System for Making Promotion and Appointment Recommendations Needs to Be Manageable

Manageability relates to the amount of human and material resources that the system requires to accomplish fully its tasks. It is preferable that written policies and procedures err on the side of clarity and completeness as compared with vagueness, yet this virtue can become a fault if the policies and procedures become so complex and detailed that they are difficult to understand and/ or to manage. An excessive number of reviews can make committee decisions more difficult and time consuming and not necessarily more equitable. One might ask, "Do our review procedures contain redundant layers of reviews?" There may be no easy answers.

New CEOs or CAOs may develop extra review stages to improve quality control of promotion and appointment process, but the creation of additional layers of review should occur only when a convincing case can be made for their value.

Committees of the whole, where an entire department or unit may sit in judgment of a colleague, also can detract from manageability. While committees may seem like the quintessence of participatory government, in some cases the decisions have been made quietly and privately beforehand and the meetings are, in essence, facades. Committees also can get out of hand without adroit leadership by the chairperson, and public airings of personal conflicts can leave deep scars that may impede future collegial relationships.

Institutions need to review periodically the deadlines for completing various phases of the personnel processes. Is sufficient time available to complete the process in a satisfactory manner? Excessive time can encourage indifference and a last-minute scramble to meet half-forgotten deadlines. Scrupulous adherence to deadlines may seem trivial, yet overlooking such details has caused major management problems and, in some cases, legal problems.

The management processes for making academic personnel decisions are designed to include essential processes and rights but not to meet every eventuality. All eventualities cannot be covered, although some professionally designed systems have tried. Just as public laws are designed to cover the majority of typical cases, so effective academic personnel policies and procedures focus on the most important matters.

An Academic Grievance Procedure Allows Recourse

A few grievance procedures have been carefully crafted to provide the form rather than the substance of recourse, but the large majority of grievance procedures have sought to provide authentic avenues for redress. To take an industrial example, IBM developed a "bypass" policy whereby an employee who believes that he or she has been unfairly evaluated by an immediate superior can bypass that person and make an appeal to an official on the next level. One IBM official told of an incident that cemented his lifelong loyalty to the company. When his immediate superior had given him a negative evaluation, he used the bypass policy to appeal to the next highest level. The immediate superior subsequently bypassed *his* superior, taking the case to yet a higher organizational level. In the end, the official was vindicated. In general, useful and equitable academic grievance procedures are based on common sense and sound legal opinion, meshed with the institution's past history and current experiences.

The Academic Personnel Decision-Making System and Its Components Are Legally Defensible

Writing on the future roles of the academic vice president, Miller (1971, p. 44) noted that "most academic deans will need sooner or later, and probably sooner, to enter the world of lawyers, legalism, and court cases." The future was here many years ago. Every two-year college should have its personnel policies and procedures checked periodically by lawyers who know general higher education laws as well as laws of a particular state.

The Overall System for Promotion and Continuing Appointments Has Reasonable Credibility

How does one judge reasonable credibility? Senior academic administrators need to listen carefully to complaints. Those who lodge the strongest complaints do not necessarily have the strongest cases, and they may take an inordinate amount of time and patience, but a careful listening process is an important aspect of credibility.

Fairness is an integral part of credibility. How does one define fairness? Certainly it is in the mind of the beholder, but it is more. While not explicitly definable in terms of a particular college, over a period of time colleges develop reputations about the fairness of their personnel policies and procedures, and particularly about their promotion and tenure system. If experienced and creative faculty members and departmental chairpersons are not generally favorable toward an established system, they probably will find ways to subtly modify the system to provide the fairness that they believe it lacks.

Three approaches may be useful in judging credibility. The nature of court cases may be one test, and comparisons with benchmark institutions may be helpful. If such comparisons show considerable variance from the mean number of serious cases at benchmark colleges, an institution would do well to review its promotion and appointment system. A second approach may include annual or biennial reviews of the institution's academic personnel policies and procedures by deans or unit chairpersons. A third approach may involve a "kitchen cabinet": a senior administrator may seek the opinions of a small group of trusted faculty members on the system's credibility.

THE ANNUAL PERFORMANCE REVIEW

All instructional staff and adjunct staff members can benefit from an Annual Performance Review (APR). The Annual Development Review (ADR) report for every staff member is one basis for making promotions and continuing appointment decisions, but colleges need additional systematic and comprehensive paper trails for making APR decisions. These processes and data can facilitate fairer, more believable, and legally defensible decision making on crucial personnel decisions. (Appendix I is one model for tracking inputs that go into making APR decisions.)

An Individualized Instructional Load (IIL)

The major data inputs that go into APR decisions are classroom teaching performance; chair evaluation; college service, including committees, classroom visitation reports, and professional growth/improvement (development); personal attributes; dean evaluation; community service/public service; professional preparation; and student advising. These activities are key inputs in the Zitlow study (1988). The final weighting of the selected criteria depends upon the missions of the institution, which can be impacted by community needs and interests; institutional, regional, and state fiscal circumstances; future college directions; needs and directions of the various departments; and the abilities and interests of individuals. Each staff member, working with the appropriate chair, crafts an individualized, weighted professional workload—an individualized instructional load (IIL).

What are the advantages and disadvantages of a numerical weighting system? There are some potential problems. For example, determining the percentage of total instructional effort can be a somewhat complex matter. If Instructor A, for example, has no advising responsibilities and does no community and/or college service, can she give zero percentage to these areas in her total professional load? What if the composition of the total professional load changes in the weighting of professional activities

Exhibit 7.1
A Conceptual Framework for Individualizing Professional
Responsibilities

	Input Groups			
Criteria	*Chair*	*Colleagues*	*Dean*	*Students*
Advising				
Administration				
Classroom visitation				
College service				
Professional service				
Professional growth				
Scholarship				
Self-evaluation				
Teaching				
Teaching Materials				

Note: Use numbers in parentheses to represent percentage weighting, words to
represent descriptive weighting.
(See Exhibits 7.2 and 7.3 for sample profiles of how the weightings and evaluations could work.)

from term to term? And could this weighted approach cause undue compartmentalization or fractionalization of professional effort so an individual might be more reluctant to undertake
activities that were outside of the IIL?

On the other hand, an IIL can provide greater clarity in describ-
ing professional responsibilities and in delineating their scope
and limits. Faculty members generally prefer clear workload expectations with specific evaluative expectations, and they also see
advantages in a system that can provide greater flexibility. Administrators generally prefer systems that have some flexibility but
usually not to the extent that is sought by faculty members.

One weighting system, a conceptual framework for individualizing professional responsibilities, is outlined in Exhibit 7.1. An
institution that uses or plans to use a weighted system should
select those activities that are compatible with the institution's
broad directional statements.

Two examples of an individually crafted professional workload

Exhibit 7.2
Performance Profile—Instructor A

Instructor _____ Year and Term _____

Chair _____ Date Completed _____

Instructor A	Percent of Total Workload	Criterion Ratings	Raw Score	Who Rates
1. Advising	10%	6.3	63	students/chair/dean
2. Classroom teaching	60	6.1	305	students/chair/self
3. College service	10	6.4	128	chair/dean/self
4. Community service	10	5.9	59	chair/dean/self
5. Professional growth	10	6.4	64	chair/self
	100%		619	

$619 \div 700 = 88\%$ is overall term rating for teaching and related activities for Instructor A.

are given. Instructor A is very busy, spending her time on a wide variety of activities. She carries enough of an advising load so that 10 percent of time is spent on it, and her teaching responsibilities are weighted for 60 percent. Being a member of an internal governance task force accounts for 10 percent (college services); chair of the annual state convention in her field for 10 percent (professional service); and she is actively pursuing some new approaches to teaching, giving 10 percent for professional growth. Her performance profile is given in Exhibit 7.2. Instructor B has a quite different profile. He is primarily a teacher with some advising, and he also chairs the college's policy committee. See Exhibit 7.3 for his profile.

Flexibility and individualization are key concepts in this system that can be tailored to the interests of the institutions as well as the individuals. For example, a college's administration can set minimums such as 10 or 15 percent for faculty development or 50 percent for teaching.

Finally, this system concludes with a "percentage of success." But some would ask "Is not an 'overall performance rating' too mechanical to suit the complexities of overall college responsibil-

Exhibit 7.3
Performance Profile—Instructor B

Instructor _____ Year and Term _____

Chair _____ Date Completed _____

Instructor B	Percent of Total Workload	Criterion Ratings	Raw Score	Who Rates
1. Advising	10%	6.2	62	students/chair/dean
2. Classroom teaching	80	6.0	480	students/chair/self
3. College service	10	5.7	57	chair/self
	100%		599	

599 ÷ 700 = 86% is overall term rating for teaching and related activities for
Instructor B.

ities, and is it not demeaning to reduce professional performance
to a percentage figure?" Current evaluation expertise does not allow one to say with any real certainty that a 90 percent rating on
overall performance is better than an 88 percent one, but one can
have more confidence in saying that a 90 percent rating is indic-
ative of better performance than a score of 84. Personnel decisions
in two-year colleges sometimes have been made on fragmentary,
excessively subjective, and second-hand information, erring on the
side of imprecision; therefore, can serious objections be raised
against a system that can bring greater sensitivity, fairness, and
precision into the overall professional evaluation process? But it
does require a commitment to significant human and material resources.

CONCLUSION

This chapter outlines a system that is more complex and more
time consuming than busy administrators would like. This view
is understandable in light of their heavy workloads and responsibilities. All of us would prefer a simpler and less complex approach to making recommendations and decisions on personnel
matters.

But our present and future simply require more detailed yet

individualized systems for providing individually fair and institutionally meaningful decisions. In each two-year college in the United States, the quality of its future will be directly linked to its academic personnel decisions. In the final analysis, faculty members with continuing appointment see deans and presidents come and go. They are the present and future of every college.

8

Moving into the Twenty-First Century

Thinking ahead of our present problems and challenges requires an ear to the past, a grasp of the present, and hopes and plans for the future. Thinking ahead also requires an optimism that the future can be better than the present. The American way of life is based upon this faith. With the myriad of today's problems and perils, the age-old American dream has been tarnished, but educators must hold to the faith that tomorrow's education can and will be better for those who follow us. This chapter provides some ideas and thoughts about the important current and professional tasks and challenges that lie ahead.

SEVEN FUTURES

State and Federal Levels of Government Need to Continue to Emphasize Quality and Evaluation

The word *quality* is a ubiquitous term to which no one objects, but it is also one that is often left undefined. State higher education agencies have over twenty years of experience and sufficient knowledge to write quality academic program policies and procedures; however, problems arise when enforcement procedures are put into place at the institutional level that call for elimination or consolidation of some instructional programs. Chief educational officers complain to their legislators who, in turn, complain to the state higher education board as well as to key higher education state government officials. Actions to reduce or eliminate instructional programs that are underenrolled, out of date, inferior, or redundant may be defeated by forces that repeat the rhetoric of cost effectiveness and quality while doing little to eliminate redundant, obsolete, or poor-quality programs.

The external clamor for better quality and more evaluation does impact institutional-level activities, partly out of fear on the part of college officials that state-level officials and politicians might actually follow up their words with action.

More Attention to Post-Tenure Review Continues to Be Needed

Some years ago the prestigious National Commission on Higher Education Issues identified post-tenure evaluation as one of the most pressing issues facing higher education in the next decade. In its summary report, the commission recommended that "campus academic administrators working closely with appropriate faculty committees should develop a system of post-tenure" (1982, p. 10). The commission also warned that "nothing will undermine the tenure system more completely than its being regarded as a system to protect faculty members from evaluation" (p. 182). The issue of post-tenure review is certainly not new, and it has even greater importance in present times of scarce fiscal resources and demands for programmatic reallocation.

The earlier mentioned survey by Andrews and Licata (1991, pp. 69–75) queried 199 two-year college administrators (vice presidents and instructional deans) in the north central accreditation region of the United States on their perceptions of existing evaluation systems. On the question, "What are the stated purposes for faculty evaluation?" they found that 55 percent said it was the "basis for faculty development"; 29 percent said it was for "making decisions on promotion, retention, and dismissal"; and 11 percent said it was for "making merit compensation or merit recognition decisions." The administrators answered in about the same way when asked, "What *should* be the purpose?" When asked about the *"effectiveness* of post-tenure evaluation," 3 percent said it was very effective, 56 percent said it was effective, 33 percent said they were "uncertain about effectiveness," and 8 percent said it was "ineffective." From these studies as well as other materials in this book and elsewhere, it is clear that senior instructional administrators will be expected in the future to give higher priority to establishing more effective and efficient faculty evaluation *systems*.

More Attention Will Focus on Developing and Evaluating Faculty Improvement Programs

The litany of platitudes acclaiming the value and importance of faculty development never seems to stop, but the rhetoric cannot replace the need for greater commitments of human and material resources to these efforts. Evaluation of faculty development programs needs to consider the amount of fiscal and human resource support the programs receive by more conventional ways of surveys and interviews.

Poorly Defined and/or Nonoperationalized Institutional Goals and Objectives Can Negatively Impact Faculty Evaluation and Development

How are institutional goals and objectives related to ongoing instructional programs and to program and staff evaluations? A college that knows where it wants to go has a better chance of getting there and also will be less threatened by fair but vigorous systems of evaluation and development, but one that does not "have its act together" probably will not have its evaluation processes together either.

Evaluation Is Everyone's Responsibility in a Dynamic College

While some individuals are more deeply involved in evaluation than others, it is really everyone's responsibility. A college can become "evaluation-happy," just as anything can be overdone, but there is not much chance of this overkill happening in most colleges. Keeping in mind the integral relations within the planning-doing (leading-managing)-evaluating circle can assist in keeping a balanced perspective (see Exhibit 1.2).

Creativity and Imagination Sometimes Are Forgotten Factors in Evaluation Systems

What Menges wrote in 1984 is equally applicable today: "Most present evaluation systems, because they are the result of compromise, are inherently conservative." More creative and imaginative thinking about our evaluation systems is needed. Surely humankind's boundless sources of creating new things have not been exhausted when it comes to personnel and programs. Maybe some mildly revolutionary thinking can nudge the evolution ahead. Who will be first?

Management Has the Key Role in Significant Improvement in Faculty Development and Evaluation Systems

W. Edwards Deming contended that 85 percent of management problems are the fault of administrators, and 15 percent are the fault of workers—in this case, faculty members (Shonebarger, 1991, p. 106). Certainly a literal translation of this postulate to higher education is not desirable, and few will dispute the view that administrators are the key to significant changes in evaluations. Working with faculty groups, key administrators are in a position to move good ideas into effective practices. It really boils down to both faculty members and administrators working cooperatively, but sometimes in quite different ways, toward a common goal of better faculty and administrator evaluation and development systems.

PLANNING FOR AND EVALUATING DISTANCE LEARNING

An issue that is certain to demand an increasing amount of discussion in the new millennium is the appropriate role of distance learning within higher education. Not surprisingly, many two-year colleges in the United States have been at the cutting edge of this innovative mode of delivering coursework. At present, colleges are implementing distance learning primarily by way of television and the computer. Specifically, the modes include:

- videotapes that can be mailed
- live video broadcasts
- delayed video broadcasts
- video teleconferencing
- Internet-delivered presentations and assignments
- Internet chat rooms
- Internet-delivered electronic mail

The phenomenal spread of distance learning throughout academe has been driven by several advantages or perceived advantages:

- It can provide access to higher education for people unable to attend traditional classes.
- It can allow learning to occur at an optimum pace.
- It can enhance learning through the incorporation of various media such as video and animation.
- It is perceived by many governors and legislators as an inexpensive means of delivering coursework.
- Student satisfaction levels can be very high.

In response to one or more of these potential benefits, many U.S. two-year colleges have initiated making coursework available by alternative modes. For example, Colorado's eleven-member system of community colleges collaborated to form a virtual twelfth school called Colorado Electronic Community College without having to construct even one building. Coursework can now be accessed asynchronously through the telecommunication or Internet media by students across or far outside of Colorado, and students can communicate with one another and the instructor by e-mail or voice mail (Susman, 1997). Whereas many people would find this kind of educational experience unfulfilling and desirable only when face-to-face interaction is impossible, many college-age students who have grown up in front of computer monitors are quite happy to interact online. Some colleges have discovered that up to 60 percent of information inquiries from students can be handled by an information system such as a web page instead of requiring a human response—and with high student satisfaction (Twigg and Oblinger, 1997). Consistent with this pattern, Colorado Electronic Community College officials report 90 percent student satisfaction with their courses and retention, and completion rates that equal or exceed campus-based students (Susman, 1997).

Of course, such a departure from the traditional classroom environment has profound implications for faculty as questions arise concerning student accountability, demands placed on faculty, compensation, and appropriateness of the delivery system to community college students. College faculty's receptivity to innovative methodologies is influenced by the perceived feasibility of the change (Finkelstein, 1984). Aside from the technological feasibility of distance learning, there is the critical issue of student accountability—or, phrased differently, how can one be sure who is actually doing the work? A review of the literature on distance learning reveals a disturbing absence of concern over student accountability, a perplexing situation when one considers that assignments and tests that are received and returned over the Internet are unproctored. In contrast, faculty who teach traditional courses are expected to proctor tests and otherwise ensure that course grades are reflective of actual learning. Because distance learning is relatively new, many educators have yet to adequately address this issue. As observed by Reed and Sork (1990), "Since there is no code of ethics in distance education, those in the field are left to . . . justify the ethics of their practice." Nonetheless, accreditation agencies and state legislatures may recognize the need for the same level of accountability in both the distance and the traditional classroom delivery modes, thereby possibly mandating greater responsibility on the part of faculty involved in distance learning and imposing another dimension to how they will be evaluated. Therefore, prudent administrators will take the initiative and ensure that faculty involved in distance learning are not designing courses that rely on the integrity of the student to complete assignments and exams without assistance.

Nielson (1997) reports that three assessment systems are being employed to ensure the quality of distance learners who have completed programs in teacher education: continuous assessment, internal examination, and external examinations. Continuous assessment requires that students can use computer-based instruction (CBI) to demonstrate a mastery of blocks of material before they can advance to the next unit or level. Internal examinations are delivered to the student and then returned to the instructor for grading. In both systems, the instructor has no way to know who is actually answering the test questions or performing the assignments. In the case of external examination systems, the student exams are administered at a location near the student where a proctor can ensure that the test score was earned under conditions prescribed by the school, thereby helping administrators to assess the instructor's efforts.

Other indicators of the quality of distance learning instruction include rates of completion, sizes of course enrollment, feedback from both students who have completed and students who have withdrawn from courses, and assessment from consultants who are hired to evaluate course design (Reed and Sork, 1990).

The assessment process for faculty members involved in distance learning needs to reflect the significantly greater amount of time involved in preparing and delivering coursework through the new technology. A special report in *Academe*, "Distance Learning: A Report" (1998), lists five areas of increased work load:

1. Distance learning requires faculty to develop expertise and preparation in technical areas apart from traditional academic educations.

2. Distance learning courses usually require greater preparation for each class session than is typical for the standard lecture class.

3. Distance learning courses involving interactive television affect time lines when faculty must prepare and distribute materials to students in advance of the class activity.

4. Instructors may need to prepare for multiple student audiences simultaneously. During one semester, an Anne Arundel Community College instructor taught the same course in three modes—traditional classroom, television, and the Web.

5. Distance learning often alters the manner in which faculty assess or evaluate student performance. The traditional chapter quizzes of the traditional classroom are inappropriate in the distance learning mode.

These assertions are reinforced by the University of Central Florida's distance learning program, which consists of both Web-based and televised classes (Cornell, 1999). Fifty-eight percent of surveyed faculty reported that distance teaching required much more work from them than does traditional teaching.

Clearly, colleges that assign distance learning courses to faculty members must support those efforts initially with adequate time and technology in order to facilitate results that can produce favorable evaluations of the instructors' efforts. Conversely, schools that encourage innovative course delivery without the appropriate investment are likely to see faculty efforts met with problems that will frustrate students, demoralize instructors saddled with poor evaluations, and discourage other faculty members from venturing into a potentially beneficial venture.

The assessment of faculty involved in distance learning as well as the nature of the coursework and its delivery can be achieved with feedback from three sources: students, faculty, and supervisors or consultants hired to review courses. Students who have completed a course can assess it relative to six criteria:

1. the quality of teaching;
2. the quality of transmission and technology;
3. availability of assistance;
4. quality of assistance;
5. quality of course offerings; and
6. course relevance to the program.

Faculty evaluative input can address five factors:

1. the quality of transmission and technology;
2. opportunities for timely student feedback and communication;
3. amenability of the technology to the stated purposes of the course;
4. availability of appropriate nonmedia resources; and
5. appropriate and meaningful evaluation.

By approaching the assessment of delivering distance education from these three perspectives, administrators should be able to form a fair and accurate evaluation process that can build toward high-quality and rigorous courses available to an otherwise un-served population and by doing so, expand the term community to encompass a much larger portion of the world.

PLANNING AHEAD

Failure to anticipate problems can provide short-term compla-cency and long-term anxiety. Sometimes ignorance can result in positive innovation because if we knew what we were getting into, we never would have undertaken some things that turn out to be some of our greatest successes! But failing to foresee weak-nesses and problems is perhaps the greatest impediment to suc-cessful change strategies. In order to better anticipate problems it is useful to consider several reasons why evaluation and devel-opment models and plans fail.

- An obvious reason, but one that we prefer to overlook, is that our models are poor ones. Our failed projects and plans in higher education are rarely acknowledged as failures. As mentioned earlier, crop failure analyses are done in agriculture and autopsies are performed in med-icine, but in higher education we just write another proposal.
- The plan is not vigorously and consistently supported at the top. Win-dow dressing support cannot provide the quiet, persistent, and creative support that must come from the top if extensive faculty personnel policies and procedures are to be developed and are to succeed.
- The plan is too complex. Adherence to the KISS theory (keep it short and sweet) can be helpful. Academics tend to err on the side of com-plexity, and complexity may be inevitable at the earlier phases of most projects; however streamlining and simplicity should become the final driving forces in order to move ideas and programs from theory to action.
- Adequate attention is not given to the relationships of ends to means and means to ends and to the *symbiotic* relationships of all of the parts so the whole becomes something greater than the sum of the parts.

NEEDS FOR THE FUTURE

Every two-year college should have an instructional staff eval-uation system. While every college has staff evaluation, an eval-uation *system* is less common. Most often a so-called system is not a system but a series of parts that are very loosely integrated if at all. The emphasis should be on system, which can be defined as a number of components, such as student ratings, classroom observation, self-evaluation such as a portfolio, and colleague evaluation that are linked together synergistically. The system also includes articulated information and instruction about administering and using the various components of the system, and about the uses of the various inputs in the promotion, permanent appointment, and annual review processes.

Faculty Evaluation Systems Should Be Designed Primarily to Improve Performance

Some individuals may believe that this guideline is more rhetoric than substance, contending that the bottom line is the use of faculty evaluation for making academic promotion and tenure decisions. If this guideline is perceived to be empty rhetoric, then the administrators probably will find that cynicism about helping individuals improve is turning creative faculty minds toward finding ways of subtly thwarting or circumventing the system.

This principle does not deny the importance of summative evaluation for making personnel decisions, but if the system has reasonable credibility among institutional staff members, then negative faculty evaluations can be seen as signals for improving performance for individuals who are performing below expectations. Or faculty evaluations can be seen as ways of improving teaching performance by replacing those teachers who have been judged to have very poor classroom performances and who are judged as having little reasonable expectations for substantial future improvement. This principle does not deny the importance of terminating the professional services of staff members who do not meet institutional standards or who find themselves in obsolete fields.

Staff Evaluation and Improvement Programs Should Be Organizationally and Operationally Linked

Officials who have prime organizational responsibility for the teaching evaluation system should be in close liaison with those who direct and/or coordinate the teaching improvement programs. In some cases it may be the same individual, but in any case these persons should have regularly scheduled meetings on teaching evaluation and improvement with the chief instructional officer. Difficulties involved in having regular meetings of the interested parties tell others something about possible gaps in communication or lack of genuine interest in these matters.

An Annual Developmental Review and an Annual Performance Review Should Be Done for Each Faculty Member Each Year

As mentioned in Chapter 6, two scheduled meetings should be held between each faculty member and the immediate supervisor, probably the chair, and these half-hour to one-hour meetings should focus on performance evaluation and on professional development over the past year. A look ahead also should be an important part of these meetings. The results of each of the two meetings need to be summarized in two separate written reports.

Consideration is given to the balance between institutional needs and individual interests, and the nature of this balance will vary. In hard economic times, institutional needs become more important *vis-à-vis* individual interests. Lincoln (1983) and others have written about "worth" and "merit" decisions, saying that the worth decisions are primarily institutional-level decisions, whereas the merit decisions are primarily professional judgments based more on an individual's academic credentials and performance and therefore should be determined by self-reporting, by professional colleagues, and the chair.

More Attention to the Processes of Creative Improvements Can Be Expected in the Future

Change for change's sake is not recommended. President Millard Fillmore pointed out in his Third Annual Address in 1847: "It is not strange . . . that such an exuberance of enterprise should cause some individuals to mistake change for progress."

Teachers tend to be more process-sensitive in terms of their instructional specialties, but this orientation may be lost upon administrators who are primarily considering managerial and organizational needs and problems. Administrators focus more on "what" rather than on "how" questions. Shepherding new evaluation and development programs through the mystical labyrinths of institutional governance requires greater awareness and sensitivity to process methods and strategies. In other words, key faculty participation must be integral to administrative decision making on evaluation and development.

IMPROVEMENT AND EVALUATION ARE ABOUT THE FUTURE

Improvement and evaluation are where institutions and individuals are going to move ahead, maintain, or fall behind. Two-year colleges give generous accolades to the importance of faculty improvement, but in the vernacular, they have not always put their money where their mouth is. Hopple's (1991) and Centra's (1976) data on faculty development and other research findings indicate that about 1 percent of the total budget is set aside for development programs as compared to 5 to 10 percent for development in the business and industrial sectors. Evaluation of two-year college development programs has had a low priority, perhaps because some administrators and others would prefer to talk positively about the results rather than to systematically address them. While very few colleges ever die, they can become ossified and of average use to their students and others unless they strive constantly to be "ahead of the curve," and that means sustained, imaginative, and well-supported faculty evaluation and improvement programs.

Epilogue

Faculty evaluation and development always should be kept in perspective. The primary mission of every two-year college is the education of young and not-so-young adults. To accomplish this mission, colleges employ faculty members to teach and administrators to administer—and many wish the realities were that simple. The substantial majority of faculty members are serious students of their respective subjects, find teaching challenging and enjoyable, and are doing a professionally competent job. This generalization does not say that improvement is not always possible; it is, and instructional staff can improve performance by seeing themselves through the eyes of others. When the purpose of one's life work is to influence others, it is altogether fitting that the views of others do count.

A small group of faculty members is doing little other than drawing their paychecks, and they have psychologically "tuned out" of the dynamism and excitement of their subject area and may even resent others who have not also done so. These instructors need encouragement and sympathetic support, and they also may need some less gentle pressures. Someone pays the salaries of college and university personnel—either federal, state, or private sources. In any case, administrators have the right to insist, and they are increasingly doing so, with positive, humane, and effective pedagogical results. Faculty evaluation can assist the administration and faculty colleagues in discerning which individuals are performing at acceptable levels—a function that should be diagnostic rather than punitive, and if the evaluation is well designed and properly administered it can be the fairest way of making sound decisions about professional performance.

Administrative evaluation is desirable and necessary, and it is neither fair nor consistent to advocate faculty evaluation without also having in place an administrator evaluation system that includes serious faculty input. Evaluation should not stop with administrators; it should be institution-wide and include support personnel and various administrative roles, and performances of coordinating and governing boards also should be accountable.

How does one measure institutional quality? Is it by the number of teacher excellence award winners, the cost-ratios of degree production, average income of graduates, contributions to professional fields, and so forth? Too little is known about these larger questions that significantly impact on institutional evaluation. Accreditation reports can be helpful, but they should be viewed as means to larger institutional ends rather than ends in themselves.

In conclusion, we would like to return to the heart of evaluating and improving faculty performance: What is good teaching and how do we measure and improve it? Philosophers and others in the golden age of Greece carried on serious dialogues about teaching and learning, and the teachers in Egyptian advanced schools during the era of Alexander the Great also discussed these matters. In the middle of the fourth century in Antioch, Asia Minor, a father suspecting his son's teacher of inferior performance had the right to have his son examined by another authority. If the examination confirmed the teacher's negligence, the father could enter a formal complaint against the teacher. If a panel of teachers and laymen confirmed the teacher's neglect, the father was permitted to transfer his fees and patronage to a new teacher.

To teachers, the ecstasy and the agony of teaching is a lifelong journey of becoming—always becoming—always seeking to ignite in others the thrill of learning, which knows no bounds of age, subject, or setting. It knows only itself. In the ancient Greek saying *Gnothi seaton* (know thyself) lies the ultimate purpose of evaluation: self-improvement through self-knowledge, which rests upon honest and continuous self-analysis and evaluation. Good teachers are always striving, sometimes falling but rising again, always moving toward higher plateaus of excellence.

Appendix A

Recommended Improvements in Evaluation

Evaluation Design Recommendations	Rank Order
1. Tie evaluation system to faculty development/to a formative purpose	1
2. Increase peer involvement/explore classroom visitation as a technique	3
3. Enhance student involvement in review through student evaluation of teaching/improve student evaluation instrumentation	5
4. Involve faculty in design and establishment of individual professional goals	9
5. Lessen importance of student evaluation	10
6. Ensure plan is consistent and systematic, decreasing possibility for subjective assessment	10
7. Include multiple resources of evaluation input	10

Evaluation Implementation Recommendations	**Rank Order**
1. Provide opportunities for training of evaluators	4
2. Decrease frequency of evaluation from yearly to a two- to three-year cycle	7
3. Establish a nonthreatening climate for evaluation	13

Evaluation Outcomes Recommendations	**Rank Order**
1. Provide incentives for excellent performers	4
2. Provide adequate resources for faculty development	5
3. Make evaluation more effective in retention/dismissal/reward	7
4. Monitor results of development plans established as a consequence of the evaluation	10

Source: Licata and Andrews, 1992.

Appendix B

Teaching/Learning Values at Miami-Dade Community College

I. **Miami-Dade Community College values learning.**

To support this value, the College:

- Creates an environment conducive to teaching and learning.
- Supports life-long learning.
- Encourages the free interchange of ideas and beliefs.
- Provides the resources necessary for teaching and learning.
- Employs qualified personnel to facilitate learning.
- Provides advisement and counseling to support the needs of students.
- Expects everyone to participate actively in the learning process.
- Addresses the learning needs of the community.
- Emphasizes communication skills.

II. **Miami-Dade Community College values change to meet educational needs and to improve learning.**

To support this value, the College:

- Encourages and supports innovation and creativity.
- Responds to the changing educational needs of the community.
- Anticipates the future needs of the community.
- Supports faculty and staff development.

III.   **Miami-Dade Community College values access while maintaining quality.**

To support this value, the College:

· Provides support services to assist students in meeting their educational goals.

· Offers students prescriptive learning opportunities.

· Provides occupational education which prepares the graduate to work at levels expected by the community.

· Expects students to meet defined standards.

· Provides academic programs which prepare the graduate to succeed in upper division learning.

· Provides educational opportunities for personal development.

· Structures the admissions process to encourage enrollment.

· Provides a variety of scholarships and financial aid programs.

IV.   **Miami-Dade Community College values diversity in order to broaden understanding and learning.**

To support this value, the College:

· Respects individuals from a variety of cultural backgrounds.

· Provides role models.

· Offers interdisciplinary educational programs.

· Provides programs and opportunities for student growth.

· Teaches students about the cultural, economic, political, and social environments in which they live.

· Helps students to understand themselves and others.

· Sponsors academic organizations and extracurricular activities.

· Respects and responds to students' different learning styles.

· Respects and accepts different teaching styles.

V.   **Miami-Dade Community College values individuals.**

To support this value, the College:

· Encourages a positive attitude toward teaching and learning.

· Stresses honesty and integrity.

· Expects all individuals to interact.

· Communicates accurately and promptly.

· Recognizes the importance of prior learning and experience.

· Develops realistic expectations for all individuals.

- Publishes explicit performance expectations for faculty, staff, and administrators.
- Publishes explicit performance expectations for students.
- Rewards achievement.

VI. **Miami-Dade Community College values a systematic approach to decision-making.**

To support this value, the College:

- Collects accurate and current data.
- Assesses the community's learning needs.
- Measures students' abilities upon entry to the institution.
- Assesses programs' effectiveness.
- Provides feedback to assist in meeting standards.
- Evaluates students' progress throughout their careers at Miami-Dade Community College.
- Encourages individuals to be aware of relevant current research.
- Surveys students' perceptions about courses, programs, and the teaching/learning environment.
- Uses the expertise of the faculty to improve the teaching/learning process.

VII. **Miami-Dade Community College values its partnership with the community.**

To support this value the College:

- Provides accessible campus and outreach centers.
- Cooperates with other educational systems.
- Supports activities that enrich the community.
- Plans educational programs with business and industry to promote the local economic development of the community.
- Increases the community's awareness of College programs and activities.

Source: Miami-Dade Community College, 1988.

Appendix C

Summary of Studies Used to Evaluate Teaching Performance

	Gustad		Astin & Lee	Centra	Seldin*		Traylor	Average
	1961	1966	1967	1979	1980	1984	1992	1961-92
Chair Evaluation	1	1	1	1	1	1	2	1
Classroom Visits	2	13	11	12	10	9	9	10
Colleagues' Opinions/ Ratings	5	3	3	2	4	6	6	5
Committee Evaluation	-	-	8	4	3	4	4	4
Course Registration	12	7	-	-	-	-	-	-
Course Syllabi & Exams	7	8	7	7	9	7	6	8
Dean Evaluation	4	2	2	6	2	3	3	2
Informal Methods	10	-	5	-	-	-	-	-

Informal Student Opinions	3	5	-	5	8	10	10	9
Long-term Follow-up of Students	8	15	14	14	14	13	12	
Scholarly Research/ Publications	-	4	4	-	7	7	5	7
Self-evaluation or Report	16	10	10	9	6	5	8	6
Student Examination Performance	9	9	9	11	11	12	11	11
Systematic Student Ratings	6	12	12	2	5	5	1	3

*The Seldin studies focused on the private sector.

Appendix D

Classroom Visitation Evaluation

Instructor_____ Course_____

Term_____ Academic Year_____

Visitor(s)_____ Title_____

        The following appraisal form contains many of the same questions that also are found on the student appraisal of classroom teaching form. In addition, you may want to develop a narrative description of your visit.

<u>Directions</u>: Please rate classroom teaching on each item. Use numbers 12 and 13 for additional questions.

Highest			Middle			Lowest	Don't Know
7	6	5	4	3	2	1	X

____ 1. Major objectives of the course were made clear to you in the written materials.

____ 2. Class presentation was effectively planned.

____ 3. Class presentation was efficiently used.

____ 4. Important ideas were explained clearly.

____ 5. Instructor had mastery of the course content.

____ 6. Teacher encouraged critical thinking and analysis.

____ 7. Instructor encouraged relevant student involvement in the classroom activities.

____ 8. Instructor reacted positively and openly to student viewpoints differing from his/her own.

____ 9.   Attitudes of students toward the teacher were positive and open minded.

____ 10. My visitation was at a time when I was able to judge fairly the nature and tenor of
          the teaching-learning processes.

____ 11. Considering the previous 10 items, this is my overall rating of this teacher.

____ 12. _____

____ 13. _____

____ 14. Considering the previous items, what is your overall rating?

Yes____ No____   Did you have a preliminary conference with the teacher before
                              the visitation?

Yes____ No____   Do you have a follow-up conference planned?

Comments after class visitation:_____

_____

Comments after follow-up conference:_____

_____

(Continue comments on back of the page if necessary.)

Appendix E

Self-Evaluation of Teaching

Teacher_____ Course_____

Term_____ Academic Year_____

      Thoughtful self-evaluation can help improve teaching effectiveness and efficiency. You are asked to evaluate your own teaching performance.

      Please use the back of this form for written comments. These might be unusual circumstances that relate to your teaching, class circumstances, and/or teaching course load. At your option, questions 12 and 13 may be added.

Directions: Rate yourself on each item, using this scale.

Highest			Middle			Lowest	Don't Know
7	6	5	4	3	2	1	X

_____ 1. The major objectives of the course were made clear in the syllabus and verbally to the students.

_____ 2. There was substantial agreement between course objectives and lesson assignments.

_____ 3. Class presentations were well planned and organized.

_____ 4. Important ideas were explained clearly.

_____ 5. My mastery of the course content was evident to the students.

_____ 6. Class time was used efficiently and effectively.

_____ 7. Student critical thinking and analyses were creatively encouraged.

_____ 8. Student viewpoints different from my own were encouraged.

_____ 9. Students were encouraged to seek my help when needed.

_____ 10. Relevant student involvement in the class and related activities was encouraged.

_____ 11. _____

_____ 12. _____

_____ 13. Considering all of the items, this is my overall rating of my teaching.

Questions and comments on back side of the page

Appendix F

Teaching Materials Evaluation

Instructor_____ Date_____

Course_____ Academic Term_____

Appraiser(s)_____ Position_____

      This appraisal form is designed to gain information about the faculty member's teaching materials and resources. Additional questions may be added. You also may want to add a summary statement in your own words.

Directions: Please rate each item on this scale.

Highest		Middle		Lowest			Don't Know
7	6	5	4	3	2	1	X

____ 1. The students can gain a coherent and comprehensive overview of the course from its outline and the related materials.

____ 2. The course materials and resources include professional materials and works from accepted authorities and sources in the field as well as providing new materials and points-of-view.

____ 3. The course's stated grading policies and procedures are reasonable in terms of course content and requirements.

____ 4. The course content, materials, and organization indicate that students can have a challenging and meaningful educational experience.

_____ 5. Based upon examining the course outline and other materials, how would you rate the course preparation by this instructor?

_____ 6. Based upon course related materials, how would you rate the overall quality of the course?

_____ 7. _____

_____ 8. _____

_____ 9. Considering all of the items, this is my overall rating.

Summary:

Appendix G

Steps to Consider in Developing a Faculty Evaluation System

I. **Establishing the Committee**

    A.   The charge and role of the committee should be clearly stated.

        1.   Whoever established the committee should clearly state what the goals and objectives are for the committee.

        2.   Key questions that either the person forming the committee, the committee itself or a combination of both will need to address are as follows:

            a)   Is the evaluation system to be:

                (1)   +-Summative.

                    (a) Personnel decisions like granting tenure, advancement, and maintaining tenure, merit, etc.

                (2)   Formative.

                    (a) Professional growth.

                (3)   Combination of both.

            b)   Is the evaluation system to include:

                (1)   Faculty going through tenure.

                (2)   Faculty going through advancement.

(3)   Merit pay.

(4)   All full-time faculty.

(5)   All part-time faculty.

(6)   Some combination of the above.

c)   Is the evaluation committee to address:

(1)   The process and procedures for faculty evaluation.

(2)   Developing the instruments for faculty evaluation.

(3)   Both.

d)   Does the committee:

(1)   Find a consultant to work with the committee.

(2)   Hire a consultant to develop a plan for the committee.

(3)   Work by itself.

(4)   Combination of above.

e)   Does the committee:

(1)   Develop its own evaluation instruments.

(2)   Use one of the many standardized instruments.

(3)   Use a combination of both.

f)   Who is responsible for writing the evaluation analysis:

(1)   Administration.

(2)   Faculty committee.

(3)   Outside evaluator.

(4)   Expert in discipline field.

(5)   Evaluee his/herself.

(6)   Some combination of above.

g)   Who should provide information for evaluating faculty:

(1)   Administration.

(2)   Peers.

(3)   Students.

(4)   Evaluee.

(5)   Expert in the field.

    (a) From inside the institution.

    (b) From outside the institution.

        (6)   Some combination of the above.

    h)   Where do the evaluation results go:

        (1)   Personnel file.

        (2)   Organization unit file.

        (3)   The evaluee.

        (4)   Combination of the above.

B.   Selection of Committee Members

    1.   Committee members should be:

        a)   Predominantly faculty.

        b)   Representing the various faculty organizational units.

        c)   Highly respected.

        d)   Task oriented.

        e)   Good communicators.

C.   Committee Organization

    1.   Determine who will chair the committee.

        a)   A written agenda should be prepared and distributed in advance of each meeting time.

        b)   The chair should guide the direction of the committee and keep it on track.

        c)   Tasks should be assigned at the end of each meeting.

        d)   The chair should do a quick re-cap at the end of the meeting.

    2.   Determine who should be secretary for the committee.

        a)   Minutes should be taken, typed and distributed to the campus committee.

    3.   The committee should determine how the minutes and other material is to be disseminated to the campus in general.

        a)   Have minutes and verbal reports given to

        (1)   The various organizational units.

        (2)   Faculty bargaining unit.

        (3)   Administration.

        (4)   Student organization.

        (5)   Classified staff.

II.   **Prepare the Committee**

    A.   Determine the committee members' opinion regarding faculty evaluation in general.

        1.   It is important to know where people are coming from.

    B.   If you have a present evaluation system determine what the opinion is of the committee members of that system.

    C.   Go over the charge and the role of the committee.

        1.   Committee members need to know what "givens" there are, if any.

        2.   Members need to know how much authority they have.

            a)   Recommendation

            b)   Decision making

        3.   Members need to know what resources are available.

        4.   Members need to know what time lines have been established, if any.

    D.   Review the mission statement and the goals and objectives of the College.

        1.   The evaluation process and procedures should be clearly tied with the mission statement and the goals and objectives of the College.

    E.   Review faculty job descriptions.

        1.   What are faculty hired to do?

        2.   Faculty evaluation should be directly linked to the job description of each faculty member.

    F.   Review the literature on faculty evaluation.

        1.   Hand out bibliography.

        2.   Provide information on what is being done with faculty evaluation.

        3.   Point out potential problems.

        4.   Provides committee with ideas.

        5.   Provides committee with background knowledge and terminology regarding faculty evaluation.

    G.   Contact other institutions and agencies that have developed faculty evaluation systems.

        1.   Gives committee creative ideas.

        2.   Provides committee with information on how other institutions are doing evaluations.

      3.   It is not a good idea to adopt another institutions' evaluation system and apply it to your own.

          a)   Does not take into consideration

              (1)   The history of your institution.

              (2)   The uniqueness of your institution both in terms of organization and its people.

H.   Consider using a consultant.

      1.   Cost can be a factor.

      2.   Need to know what the consultant can do for you.

      3.   A consultant can

          a)   Get the committee going.

          b)   Provide the committee some direction.

          c)   Help provide organization for the committee.

          d)   Provide the committee with useful ideas and suggestions.

          e)   Provide the committee with feedback on proposals generated by committee.

          f)   Can develop a proposed evaluation system.

III.   **Assumptions Regarding Faculty Evaluations Should Be Clearly Stated**

    A.   Assumptions regarding faculty evaluation should be identified and clearly stated at the beginning.

      1.   There are the premises by which the committee will be working with from the start.

      2.   They should be mutually agreed upon.

IV.   **Define the Purposes of Faculty Evaluation**

    A.   What is the purpose of faculty evaluation?

    B.   Is the purpose to:

      1.   Enhance professional growth and performance?

      2.   Attain tenure?

      3.   Maintain tenure?

      4.   Obtain advancement?

      5.   Decide merit increases?

      6.   Etc.?

V.   **Determine Specific Objectives**

A.   The committee needs to specify exactly what the objectives of the evaluation system are.

B.   For example, the objectives were to:

1.   Recognize those faculty who are performing in an outstanding
manner.

2.   Recognize individuals who are performing at a satisfactory level.

3.   Identify individuals who need or desire assistance with aspects of
their job.

4.   Provide an adequate and sound basis for personnel decisions.

C.   Under personnel decisions such actions as the following could be considered:

D.   Granting tenure.

E.   Removing tenure.

F.   Granting advancement.

G.   Allocating merit pay increases.

H.   To determine rank such as lecturer, assistant professor, associated professor, professor.

I.   Etc.

VI.   **Determine the Areas of Faculty Evaluation**

A.   What is to be measured, rated, or examined when evaluating a faculty
member?

B.   In other words, on what bases are faculty to be evaluated? What are faculty expected to do?

C.   To determine this you need to have a clear understanding of the college's
mission statement, the goals and objectives of the college and the various
job descriptions of the faculty.

D.   For BCC we determined and defined the following areas that faculty are
expected to do:

1.   Teaching/counseling/librarianship.

2.   Advising.

3.   Service to the college.

4.   Professional development.

5.   Service to the community.

VII. Establish the Criteria for the Various Areas Chosen for Faculty Evaluation

    A.   Once the areas have been determined the committee will need to determine what criteria will be used for each area.

    B.   Go back to each area and just start listing possible criteria.

        1.   Criteria can be revised, deleted, or new ones added as you go through this process.

VIII. Develop Instruments That Will Obtain Needed Information on the Criteria Established for Each Area

    A.   The committee will need to determine who shall provide information in the evaluation process and what instruments are needed to obtain that information.

    B.   The committee will then need to decide if it should construct its own instruments, use ones already established, or a combination of both.

        1.   Advantages of using instruments already developed versus developing your own:

            a)   Might be more reliable and valid.

            b)   Large number of evaluations taken to compare to.

            c)   Can compare faculty in one discipline to other like disciplines from other colleges.

            d)   Provide better statistical information.

            e)   No headache of developing your own.

        2.   Disadvantages of using standard instruments already developed versus developing your own:

            a)   There is usually a cost factor involved.

            b)   May not be able to measure all the things you wish to measure.

            c)   Does not consider the uniqueness of the institution.

            d)   Does not take into account the history of the institution.

            e)   No ownership in the instruments is established.

            f)   More difficult to bring about changes in the instruments.

            g)   Less flexibility.

    C.   Some things to consider if you develop your own instruments:

        1.   Determine the instruments that you want to use.

        2.   Assign members of the committee to develop rough drafts of the instruments.

a) For example, librarians should work on the development of a library faculty evaluation.

b) Teaching faculty should work on a student rating form.

c) Administrators should work on an administrative evaluation form of faculty and so on.

3. Need to decide if:

a) The same criteria should be applied to all instruments.

b) Different criteria should be developed for each criterion.

c) A combination of a and b should be used.

d) A rating scale type questionnaire should be used.

(1) If so, what type of rating scale?

(a) Numbers.

(b) Description.

(c) Letters.

(d) Etc.

e) Open-ended questions should be used.

f) Individuals should develop their own specific questions.

g) You should use some combination of d, e, and f.

4. In developing the student rating forms you will need to determine if you will develop one standard evaluation form for all types of teaching modes or several, depending on the type of instructional setting.

5. Need to determine the length of instruments.

a) Should not be too long.

6. If you decide to develop several evaluation instruments you will need to determine which criteria will be appropriate for each instrument.

a) Need to decide which evaluator—student, peer, self, administrator, etc.—can best provide the information needed.

(1) At BCC we used a worksheet to help determine what criteria we wanted to use, the source of information and the standards to use.

(a) Show worksheet overlay.

7. At BCC the following instruments were developed by the commit-
    tee.

    a) A faculty self-evaluation form.

    b) A peer evaluation form.

    c) An administrator evaluation form.

    d) Student evaluation forms:

        (1) A lecture/discussion form.

        (2) A lab/clinical form.

        (3) A counselors form.

        (4) A librarians form.

    e) Administrator Evaluation Statement.

IX. **Develop Process and Procedures For The Faculty Evaluation System**

  A. Determine who is to be evaluated.

    1. Faculty obtaining tenure.

    2. Faculty seeking advancement.

    3. All full-time faculty.

    4. All part-time faculty.

    5. For merit pay.

    6. For position advancement.

    7. Some combination above.

  B. Determine who shall provide information in the evaluation process and how
it shall be provided.

    1. Administrator(s).

    2. Peers.

    3. Students.

    4. Staff.

    5. Experts in the field of doing evaluation.

    6. Experts in discipline area.

        a) Inside college.

        b) Outside college.

    7. Self-evaluation.

    8. Some combination of the above.

  C. Determine who is responsible for analyzing and writing the evaluation
summary.

       1.   Administrator.

       2.   Peers.

       3.   Expert in conducting evaluations.

       4.   Expert in discipline area.

       5.   Self.

       6.   Combination of above.

D.   Determine when faculty evaluation is to take place.

       1.   How often?

           a)   Annually.

           b)   Every two years.

           c)   Etc.

       2.   During the evaluation period.

           a)   When are the data to be collected?

           b)   What forms are to be used?

           c)   When is preliminary analysis and summary to be done?

           d)   When does the interview with the evaluee take place and by whom?

           e)   When is the final analysis and summary to be completed?

           f)   Where should the final document go?

                (1)   Personnel file.

                (2)   Organizational Unit file.

                (3)   To evaluee.

                (4)   Etc.

                (5)   A combination of the above.

E.   A committee member or a few members should be responsible for writing the first rough draft of the process and procedures.

       1.   Need to get it off the ground.

       2.   Need consistency in its development.

       3.   Will probably be the most controversial part of the document.

F.   At BCC the committee chair took the responsibility to write the first rough draft of the process and procedures for:

       1.   Tenure.

       2.   Advancement.

       3.   All full-time faculty in the last advancement column or not in the tenure or advancement process.

X.   Develop Standards (Achievement Level) and Weights for Faculty Evaluation

A.   Develop standards for the various areas of faculty evaluation.

B.   Develop standards for the various criteria used in the instruments.

C.   Place weights on the areas.

    1.   For example, what percent of the total weight of evaluation should be placed on

        a)   Teaching.

        b)   Advising.

        c)   Professional growth.

        d)   Service to the college.

        e)   Service to the community.

    2.   How much weight should be placed upon each of the criteria?

        a)   Are some criteria more important than others or are they all of the same value?

    3.   Determine how much weight will be given to the various instruments used in the evaluation process.

        a)   For example, what percent of weight should be given to:

            (1)   Self-evaluation.

            (2)   Peer evaluations.

            (3)   Administrator evaluation.

            (4)   Student evaluations.

D.   At BCC we decided not to place specific weights for the evaluation process.

XI.   Develop a Grievance Procedure

A.   A grievance procedure should be established so faculty can grieve the evaluation outcomes.

B.   Grievances should be limited to arbitrary, capricious or discriminatory action on the part of the evaluator(s).

C.   Grievances should be directed above the individual who wrote the final evaluation analysis.

D.   Time lines to the grievance procedure should be clearly defined.

E.   A final step in the grievance process should be determined.

XII.   Distribute Proposed Plan and Obtain Feedback

A.   Up to this point, information on the committee's work should have been provided on a continual basis to the campus community.

          1.   Thus, proposed evaluation plan should not be a complete shock to the campus community.

    B.   Steps to consider in distributing proposed plan.

          1.   Copies of the proposed plan should be given to the campus community in advance of any meetings or hearings.

          2.   A cover letter should accompany the document to explain:

                a)   What the committee has done.

                b)   What it wants the reader to do.

                c)   How the reader can provide his/her feedback to the committee.

                d)   What are the time lines for giving his/her feedback and to whom it should be given.

    C.   Ways to obtain feedback.

          1.   Just have campus community provide written feedback upon reading the document.

          2.   Hold a general faculty meeting(s) in order to obtain verbal feedback.

          3.   Hold organizational unit meeting(s) in order to obtain verbal feedback.

          4.   Hold open hearings.

          5.   Some combination of the above.

    D.   Things to consider when meeting with campus community.

          1.   Do not argue with people who make suggestions.

          2.   Listen to concerns and write them down.

          3.   Tell faculty that their suggestions will be addressed by the committee when it revises the document.

          4.   Do not promise to make changes.

                a)   Evaluate the suggestions on their own merits.

          5.   Do not have full committee present.

                a)   If full committee is present then faculty will expect that their suggestions be acted upon right then.

XIII.   Review All Verbal and Written Feedback and Make Necessary Changes

    A.   The committee should examine all recommended changes and then determine if they should be incorporated or not.

    B.   Rewrite the document.

XIV. **Distribute Revised Proposal and Obtain Feedback**

    A.   Follow same procedure as in point number XII.

    B.   It is important that you show the campus community that you have listened to their concerns and made changes.

    C.   It is also important to let faculty have another chance to make suggested changes in the plan.

        1.   The revised document may have changed substantially from the original.

        2.   Faculty have been given another chance to make their suggested changes which were not incorporated in the revised document.

        3.   Faculty have had time to sit back and think about the evaluation process for a time and now might have some suggestions they originally didn't have.

XV. **Review Feedback and Prepare Final Document**

    A.   You are probably only looking at minor changes.

    B.   At this point there should be no substantial changes.

XVI. **Distribute the Final Document**

    A.   At BCC we took the following actions in providing information to the campus community.

        1.   Published minutes.

        2.   Individual members provided information to the various organizational units on a regular basis.

            a)   Provided ideas the committee were thinking of and bringing faculty concerns back to the committee.

        3.   The chair of the faculty evaluation task force met several times with the Dean of Instruction to provide information and salient feedback.

            a)   All faculty report to the Dean of Instruction.

        4.   The chair of the faculty evaluation task force met several times with the Instructional Cabinet.

            a)   He was a member of the cabinet.

            b)   Instructional cabinet members consist of all administrators reporting to the Dean of Instruction.

        5.   Meet with the faculty association to present ideas and to listen to their concerns.

    a)   Tried to get an executive member of the association to be a member of the faculty evaluation task force.

6.   When it came time to distribute the proposed plan itself and obtain feedback, the committee did it in a series of stages.

    a)   First, the committee distributed the first rough draft of the assumptions, purpose specific objectives, the areas of evaluation the criteria and their instruments.

        (1)   Sent out with cover letter which stated feedback could be provided in writing or verbally.

        (2)   Committee members were encouraged to meet with their respective organizational units to go over the document and answer questions.

        (3)   A series of open hearings were scheduled.

        (4)   A date was set when all feedback was to be returned to the committee.

        (5)   The committee wanted to separate the issue of the instruments from the process and procedures.

    b)   As the campus community was reading the document and attending the hearings the committee prepared the rough draft of the process and procedures for tenure, advancement and evaluation of faculty.

    c)   After the hearings were completed regarding the instruments, etc., the committee distributed a copy of the proposed plan for the process and procedures for faculty evaluation.

        (1)   The same process to obtain needed feedback was used as in the distribution of the instruments, etc.

    d)   While the campus community was reading and reacting to the process and procedures, the committee examined all recommendations and proceeded to revise the assumptions, purpose, specific objectives, the areas of faculty evaluation, the criteria, and the evaluation instruments.

B.   Upon the completion of the hearings on the process and procedures of evaluation the committee reviewed all recommendations and made revisions where necessary.

    C.   A complete second draft of the proposal on faculty evaluation was distributed across campus.

        1.   This included the process and procedures as well as the assumptions, purpose, specific objectives, areas of evaluation and the instruments.

        2.   The same process for obtaining feedback was used as in the above process.

        3.   The committee examined all recommendations and prepared the final draft proposal for faculty evaluation.

    D.   A copy of the final recommended proposal on faculty evaluation was sent to the Dean of Instruction and to the President of the Faculty Association for consideration.

    E.   It should be pointed out that the committee always worked toward consensus approval in the development of the final product.

XVII.   Develop Plan To Review The Evaluation System For The Next Few Years

    A.   Any new system will have "bugs" that will need to be worked out.

        1.   Conditions also change with time.

    B.   Therefore, there is a need to have a committee monitoring the evaluation system and to make recommended changes where needed.

XVIII. Develop a Plan to Link Faculty Evaluation and Faculty Development

    A.   Faculty evaluation and faculty development seek the same goals—improve faculty performance.

    B.   It is important to link faculty evaluation and faculty development.

    C.   Faculty development should be directly tied to the areas and criteria of faculty evaluation.

        1.   For example, if a syllabus is required of all teaching faculty as part of the evaluation process then the faculty development committee should provide workshops, seminars, or printed materials which will show the instructor how to develop a good syllabus.

    D.   If weaknesses are shown in a faculty member's evaluation, faculty development should provide a means to help that person address those weaknesses.

    E.   Likewise, if a person is evaluated as doing an outstanding job then faculty development should provide a means where she/he can continue to grow.

    F.   Without faculty evaluation and faculty development being closely linked together the probability is high that both will fail.

1.   Another important ingredient to successful faculty evaluation and faculty development is the campus community having a good working climate.

2.   It is also important that the institution provide the necessary resources, dollars, to make both faculty evaluation and faculty development viable.

XIX.   Provide Adequate Training for Personnel That Will Implement the Evaluation Process and Procedures

A.   Consider having training sessions for faculty that will be going through the evaluation process.

1.   They need to clearly understand how the system works, what will happen, what is expected of them, etc.

B.   It is important to provide training for those individuals responsible for writing the evaluation.

1.   There are potential legal implications involved.

2.   There is a correct and incorrect way to do interviews.

3.   There are correct and incorrect ways to write an evaluation assessment.

C.   Faculty development or training should be available for those people who do the self-evaluation, peer evaluation, administrative evaluations.

1.   If you leave space on the student evaluation form for faculty to add their own questions, then training should be provided to them for constructing the questions.

D.   Consider a training session for the faculty development committee.

1.   They need to know in what ways they can help the faculty evaluation effort.

XX.   Don't Get Involved Unless You Are Willing to Put a Considerable Amount of Time and Effort into this Endeavor

A.   Administration must be committed to faculty evaluation.

B.   Faculty must also see a value in developing an evaluation process.

C.   Resources must be made available to develop the evaluation system.

D.   Committee members must be willing to give a considerable amount of time and effort in developing an evaluation proposal.

This model is used through the courtesy of Bellevue Community College (BCC), Bellevue, Washington.

Appendix H

Principles of Learning

PURPOSE

The purpose of this survey is to help carry out the primary responsibilities of the Faculty Excellence Subcommittee of the steering committee for the teaching/learning project. Our basic task is to describe those behaviors that occur throughout the institution by faculty and staff, primarily by faculty, which enhance student learning.

We began by identifying several principles know to foster student learning and development. Then, we constructed several statements that reflect each principle. Those statements constitute the items in this survey.

The items are intended to cover a wide array of functions, both inside and outside the classroom. Even though a particular item may not apply to every discipline, please let your answer indicate in general the degree of importance of the item to you. We anticipate that information received from this trial run will result in some refinement and re-thinking of the items.

DIRECTIONS

Please make a judgment regarding those activities which most enhance student learning: rank each item on a scale of one to five (low to high respectively). In addition to responding to each item, please make comments if you like.

Please circle your response for each item: "1" is the lowest rank, "5" is the highest rank.

Low/High   EXCELLENT FACULTY MEMBERS AT M-DCC

1 2 3 4 5 Encourage questions from students.

1 2 3 4 5 Review answers to test questions.

1 2 3 4 5 Allow students to take courses out of the ordinary sequence.

1 2 3 4 5 Provide initial opportunities for success.

1 2 3 4 5 Show how principles can be used to remember facts and facts can be used to remember principles.

1 2 3 4 5 Use reinforcement that is appropriate to the learning situation.

1 2 3 4 5 Use examples to show students how to apply what they have learned to situations outside the classroom.

1 2 3 4 5 Use several methods to assess student learning.

1 2 3 4 5 Encourage students to approach them, thereby reducing student anxieties.

1 2 3 4 5 Maintain high performance goals for themselves.

1 2 3 4 5 Encourage students to do independent research in the library.

1 2 3 4 5 Return tests, reports, papers, etc. to students in a timely manner.

1 2 3 4 5 Grant credit for topics of interest to students, provided they are within the framework of the course.

1 2 3 4 5 Promote and encourage participation in cultural activities.

1 2 3 4 5 Ask students to go through the steps of an experiment mentally before actually performing the experiments.

1 2 3 4 5 Point out relationships between previous concepts and material currently being presented.

1 2 3 4 5 Allow students to write on topics that deviate from the original assignment (after discussion with the instructor).

1 2 3 4 5 Emphasize ideas, principles, and theories as well as facts.

1 2 3 4 5 Select strategies that are appropriate to the level of student learning/motivations.

1 2 3 4 5 Restate major concepts assigning different modalities of expression.

1 2 3 4 5 Review test items with students to clarify what has been learned.

1 2 3 4 5 Use appropriate techniques to reduce anxiety in testing situations.

1 2 3 4 5 Encourage students to set high performance goals for themselves.

1 2 3 4 5 Encourage students to relate subject matter to personal experiences.

1 2 3 4 5 Provide constructive advice to students with regard to their proposed course selection.

1 2 3 4 5 Allow students to select articles from a referenced list of topics.

1 2 3 4 5 Allow students to write about or to present material related to their own culture.

1 2 3 4 5 Explain correct responses by using examples.

1 2 3 4 5 Build a framework for students to progress from observations to conclusions.

1 2 3 4 5 Invite guest speakers and demonstrators.

1 2 3 4 5 Encourage students to learn through outside activities such as field trips.

1 2 3 4 5 Provide exercises and assignments which relate to specific careers.

1 2 3 4 5 Provide assessment devices that measure what was taught in the classroom.

1 2 3 4 5 Encourage students to learn and to use relaxation techniques to deal with anxiety.

1 2 3 4 5 Encourage and promote discussion of how society views and values the subject-matter being taught.

1 2 3 4 5 Re-evaluate student learning as a result of instructor feedback.

1 2 3 4 5 Explain evaluation system to students.

Source: Miami-Dade Community College, 1987.

Appendix I

Annual Performance Review

SUPERVISOR/CHAIR   DATE

FACULTY MEMBER   DEAN/CHAIR

Review of the Previous Year

Teaching Load: heavy-average-light

    Comments:

I.   TEACHING EFFECTIVENESS

        A.   Systematic student feedback from rating form

              Composite rating for each course

              <u>FALL COURSES</u>   COMPOSITE RATINGS:

              1.

              2.

              3.

              4.

              5.

                              Overall Rating:

Comments:

B.   Self-evaluation of teaching: summary

C.   Committee summary of teaching effectiveness:

D.   Chair summary on teaching effectiveness:

A.   Systematic student feedback from rating form
         Composite rating for each course
         <u>WINTER COURSES</u>   COMPOSITE RATINGS:
         1.
         2.
         3.
         4.
         5.
                                          Overall Rating:

Comments:

B.   Self-evaluation of teaching: summary

C.   Committee summary of teaching effectiveness:

D.   Chair summary on teaching effectiveness:

A.   Systematic student feedback from rating form

Composite rating for each course

<u>SPRING COURSES</u>   COMPOSITE RATINGS:

1.

2.

3.

4.

5.

Overall Rating:

Comments:

B.   Self-evaluation of teaching: summary

C.   Committee summary of teaching effectiveness:

D.   Chair summary on teaching effectiveness:

II.   CLASSROOM VISITATION   COMPOSITE RATINGS:

1.

2.

3.

Overall Rating:

A.   Summary

B.   Self-evaluation of visitations

C.   Committee/visitors

D.   Chair summary of classroom visitation; including strengths; areas for improvement

III.   COLLEGE SERVICE, INCLUDING COLLEGE COMMITTEES (Community service is later.)

                                                                                                Composite Ratings:

1.

2.

3.

A.   Summary

B.   Self-evaluation

C.   Appropriate others

D.   Chair summary on college/professional service; including strengths; areas for improvement

IV.   PERSONAL ATTRIBUTES

                                                                                                Composite Ratings:

1.

2.

3.

                                                                                                Overall Rating:

Chair summary on personal attributes, including strengths and areas for improvement

V.   STUDENT ADVISING

     A.   Systematic student feedback: summary

     B.   Self-evaluation of advising: comments

     C.   Colleague or Committee feedback: summary

     D.   Chair summary on student advising

VI.   COMMUNITY SERVICE

                              Composite Ratings:

     1.
     2.
     3.
                              Overall Rating:

     A.   Summary

     B.   Self-evaluation of community service

     C.   Committee evaluation

     D.   Chair summary on community service

                              Overall rating:

VII.   PROFESSIONAL SERVICE (presentation, printed materials, etc.)

Composite Ratings:

1.
2.
3.

Overall Rating:

A.   Summary

B.   Self-evaluation of professional service

C.   Committee evaluation

D.   Chair summary on professional service

VIII.   PROFESSIONAL DEVELOPMENT (improvement)

A.   Activities

B.   Self-evaluation

C.   Chair summary and evaluation

Overall rating:

OVERALL PERFORMANCE RATINGS

I.   Teaching Effectiveness

Fall courses overall rating
Winter courses overall rating
Spring courses overall rating
Summer courses overall rating
Overall yearly rating

II.   Classroom Visitations

Visit One
Visit Two
Visit Three
Overall rating

III.   College Service

Overall rating

IV.   Personal Attributes

Fall rating
Winter rating
Spring rating
Summer rating
Overall rating

V.   Student Advising

Fall rating
Winter rating
Spring rating
Summer rating
Overall rating

VI.   Community Service

           Fall rating
           Winter rating
           Spring rating
           Summer rating
           Overall rating

VII.   Professional Service

           Fall rating
           Winter rating
           Spring rating
           Summer rating
           Overall rating

VIII.   Professional Development

           Overall rating

References

Adams, W. "The State of Higher Education: Myths and Realities." *AAUP Bulletin*, 1974, 60, 119–125.

Aleamoni, L. M. "Student Ratings of Instruction." In J. Millman (ed.), *Handbook of Teacher Evaluation*. Newburg Park, CA: Sage, 1981.

Aleamoni, L. M. "Typical Faculty Concerns about Student Evaluation." *National Association of Colleges and Teachers of Agriculture Journal*, 1976, 20 (1), 16–21.

Aleamoni, L. M., and Thomas, G. S. "Differential Relationships of Student, Instructor, and Course Characteristics to General and Specific Items on a Course Questionnaire." *Teaching of Psychology*, 1980, 7 (4), 233–235.

Alfred, R. L., and Linder, V. P. "Rhetoric to Reality: Effectiveness in Community Colleges." In D. Wallen and others, *Effectiveness and Student Access: Transforming Community Colleges for the 1990s*. Conference Proceedings, 1990 (ERIC Document Reproduction Service No. ED 355–088).

Alfred, R. L., Peterson, R. O., and White, T. H. *Making Community Colleges More Effective: Leading Through Student Success*. Ann Arbor, MI: Community College Consortium, 1992 (ERIC Document Reproduction Service No. ED 354–933).

American Association of Community and Junior Colleges. *Building Communities: A Vision for a New Century: A Report of the Commission on the Future of the Community College*. Washington, DC: American Association of Community and Junior Colleges, 1988.

American Association of University Professors. Committee on Academic Freedom and Academic Tenure. "General Report of the Committee." *AAUP Bulletin*, 1915, 1, 41–42.

American Council on Education. *Campus Trends, 1996.* Washington, DC: American Council on Education, 1996.

Andrews, H. A. *Evaluating for Excellence.* Stillwater, OK: New Forums Press, Inc., 1985.

Andrews, H. A. "Expanding Merit Recognition Plans in Community Colleges." *Community College Review,* 1993, 20 (1), 50–58.

Andrews, H. A., and Licata, C. M. "Administrative Perceptions of Existing Evaluation Systems." *Journal of Personnel Evaluation in Education,* 1991, 5 (1), 69–76.

Arreola, R. A. *Developing a Comprehensive Faculty Evaluation System.* Bolton, MA: Anker Publishing Co., 1995.

Astin, A. W. *Academic Gamesmanship: Student-Oriented Change in Higher Education.* New York: Praeger, 1976.

Astin, A. W., and Lee, C.B.T. "Current Practices in Evaluation and Training of College Teachers." *The Educational Record,* 1996, 47, 361–365.

Avakian, A. N. "Conflicting Demands for Adjunct Faculty." *Community College Journal,* 1995, 65, 34–36.

Bacon, F. *Essays.* London: Dent, 1906.

Beno, B., and Smith, C. "A Guide to Staff Development Evaluation." Mission Viejo, CA: League for Innovation in the Community College, 1993.

Biles, G. E., and Tuckman, H. P. *Part-Time Faculty Personnel Management Policies.* New York: Macmillan Publishing Company, 1986.

Bilson, B. "Unrealistic Teaching Loads and Threatened Literature Courses: Or, Why We Need an MLA Community College Commission." *ADE Bulletin,* 1986, 83, 1–5.

Bowen, H. R. "Systems Theory, Excellence, and Values: Will They Mix?" Address to the Annual Meeting of the American Association for Higher Education, 1976a.

Bowen, H. R. "Where Numbers Fail." In D. M. Vermilye (ed.), *Individualizing the Systems: Current Issues in Higher Education.* San Francisco: Jossey-Bass, 1976b.

Boyer, C. M., and Lewis, D. R. *And on the Seventh Day: Faculty Consulting and Supplemental Income.* ASHE-ERIC Higher Education Report No. 3. Washington, DC: Association for the Study of Higher Education, 1985.

Boyer, E. L. *Scholarship Reconsidered: Priorities of the Professorate.* Princeton, NJ: Carnegie Foundation for the Advancement of Teaching, 1997.

Braskamp, L. A., and Ory, J. C. *Assessing Faculty Work: Enhancing Individual and Instructional Practice.* San Francisco: Jossey-Bass Publishers, 1994.

Brinko, K. T. "The Practice of Giving Feedback to Improve Teaching: What Is Effective?" *The Journal of Higher Education,* 1993, 64 (5), 574–593.

Brown, C. M., and Rector, L. M. "Evaluating Part-Time Faculty Members." In R. I. Miller (ed.), *Evaluating Major Components of Two-Year Colleges.* Washington, DC: College and University Personnel Association, 1988.

Carnegie Council on Policy Studies in Higher Education. *Three Thousand Futures: The Next Twenty Years for Higher Education.* San Francisco: Jossey-Bass, 1980.

Carter, D. J. "The Status of Faculty in Community Colleges: What Do We Know?" In W. B. Harvey and J. Valadez (eds.), *Creating and Maintaining a Diverse Faculty.* New Directions in Community Colleges, Number 87, Fall 1994, pp. 3–18.

Centra, J. A. *Determining Faculty Effectiveness.* San Francisco: Jossey-Bass, 1979.

Centra, J. A. *Faculty Development Practices in U.S. Colleges and Universities* (Project 76–30). Princeton, NJ: Educational Testing Services, 1976 (ERIC Document Reproduction Service No. ED 141–382).

Centra, J. A. *Item Reliabilities, the Factor Structure, Comparison with Alumni Ratings.* Student Instructional Report No. 3. Princeton, NJ: Educational Testing Service, 1973.

Centra, J. A. *Reflective Faculty Evaluation: Enhancing Teaching and Faculty Effectiveness.* San Francisco: Jossey-Bass Publishers, 1993.

Centra, J. A., and Creech, F. R. *The Relationship Between Student, Teacher, and Course Characteristics and Student Ratings of Teacher Effectiveness* (Project Report 76–1). Princeton, NJ: Educational Testing Services, 1976.

The Chronicle of Higher Education. "The Nation," September 1, 1994, p. 8.

Cohen, A. M. "The Constancy of Community Colleges." *On the Horizon,* 1997, 5 (1), 4–6.

Cohen, A. M., and Brawer, F. B. *The American Community College* (2nd ed.). San Francisco: Jossey-Bass, 1989.

Cohen, A. M., and Brawer, F. B. and associates. "The Challenging Environment: Context, Concepts, and Crises." In A. M. Cohen and F. B. Brawer and associates, *Managing Community Colleges.* San Francisco: Jossey-Bass, 1994.

College and University Personnel Association. "Tenure and Retrenchment Practices in Higher Education—A Technical Report." *Journal of the College and University Personnel Association,* 1980a, 31 (3–4), 18–36.

Community College Press, AACC Annual, 1997–98. *A State-by-State Analysis of Community College Trends and Statistics.* Washington, DC: Community College Press, 1977.

Cornell, R. "The Onrush of Technology in Education: The Professor's New Dilemma." *Educational Technology,* 1999, 39 (3), 60–64.

Costin, L., and associates. "Student Ratings of College Teaching: Reliability, Validity, and Usefulness." *Review of Educational Research*, 1971, 41, 511–535.

Davis, W. "Early Academic Warning System." In B. Beckman (ed.), *How to Do More With Less: Community College Innovations to Increase Efficiency and Reduce Costs*. Mission Viejo, CA: League for Innovation in the Community College, June 1996.

Diamond, R. M. "How to Change the Faculty Reward System." *Trusteeship*, 1993, 1, 17–21.

Diener, T. *Growth of an American Invention: A Documentary History of the Junior and Community College Movement*. Contributions to the Study of Education, No. 16. Westport, CT: Greenwood Press, 1986.

"Distance Learning: A Report." *Academe*, 1998, 84 (3), 30–38.

Dressel, P. L. *Handbook of Academic Evaluation*. San Francisco: Jossey-Bass, 1976.

Erwin, J., and Andrews, H. A. "State of Part-Time Faculty Services at Community Colleges in a Nineteen-State Region." *Community College Journal of Research and Practice*, 1993, 17, 555–562.

Ewell, P. T. "Effectiveness and Student Success in Community Colleges: Practices, Realities, and Imperatives." In D. Walleri and others, *Effectiveness and Student Access: Transforming Community Colleges for the 1990s*. Conference Proceedings, 1989 (ERIC Document Reproduction Service No. ED 355–088).

Feldman, K. A. "The Perceived Instructional Effectiveness of College Teachers as Related to Their Personality and Attitudinal Characteristics: A Review and Synthesis." *Research in Higher Education*, 1986, 24 (2).

Feldman, K. A. "Seniority and Experience of College Teachers as Related to Evaluations They Receive from Their Students." *Research in Higher Education*, 1983, 18 (1), 3–124.

Finkelstein, M. J. *The American Academic Profession*. Columbus: The Ohio State University Press, 1984.

Finley, C. E. "The Relationship Between Unionization and Job Satisfaction Among Two-Year College Faculty." *Community College Review*, 1991, 19 (1), 53–60.

Friedman, P. G., and Yarbrough, E. A. *Training Strategies from Start to Finish*. Englewood Cliffs, NJ: Prentice-Hall, 1985.

Gage, N. L. "The Appraisal of College Teaching." *Journal of Higher Education*, 1970, 1 (32), 17–22.

Gappa, J. M., and Leslie, D. W. *The Invisible Faculty: Improving the Status of Part-Timers in Higher Education*. San Francisco: Jossey-Bass Publishers, 1993.

Gleason, M. "Getting a Perspective on Student Evaluation." *AAHE Bulletin*, 1986, 38 (6), 10–13.

Graber, J. S. "Improving Connections with New Adjunct Faculty." *Adjunct Info*, 1997, 5, 3.

Grymes, R. J., Jr. *A Survey and Analysis of Part-Time Instructors at J. Sargent Reynolds Community College.* Richmond, VA: J. Reynolds Community College, 1976 (ERIC Document Reproduction Service No. ED 125–687).

Gustad, J. W. "Evaluation of Teaching Performance: Issues and Possibilities." In C.B.T. Lee (ed.), *Improving College Teaching.* Washington, DC: American Council on Education, 1967.

Gustad, J. W. *Policies and Practices in Faculty Evaluation.* Washington, DC: American Council on Education, Committee on College Teaching, 1961.

Hammons, J. O. "Faculty Development: A Necessary Corollary to Faculty Evaluation." In A. B. Smith (ed.), *Evaluating Faculty and Staff,* New Directions for Community Colleges, No. 41, pp. 75–82. San Francisco: Jossey-Bass, 1983.

Hammons, J. O. "Staff Development Isn't Enough." *Community College Review,* 1983, 10 (3), 3–7.

Hammons, J. O., and Barnsley, J. R. "The Elusive Search to Define the Effective Community College Teacher." *Community College Journal of Research and Practice,* 1996, 20, 311–324.

Hammons, J. O., and Murrey, A. F., Jr. "Management Appraisal Systems in Community Colleges: How Good Are They?" *Community College Review,* 1983, 24, 19–28.

Hammons, J. O., and others. *Staff Development in the Community College: A Handbook, Topical Paper No. 66.* Los Angeles: ERIC Clearinghouse for Junior Colleges, UCLA, 1978 (ERIC Document Reproduction Service No. ED 154–887).

Hefferlin, J. B. *Dynamics of Academic Reform.* San Francisco: Jossey-Bass, 1969.

"Heisenberg, W." *The World Book Encyclopedia,* vol. 9. Chicago: World Book, 1967, 159.

Highet, G. *The Art of Teaching.* New York: Vintage/Random House, 1950, 1989.

Hopple, T. G. *Professional Faculty Development Practices Used in Two-Year Postsecondary Educational Institutions.* Unpublished doctoral dissertation, Ohio University, 1991.

Jervis, J. L. "The Ideal Academy." *Trusteeship,* 1995, 3, 22–25.

Julius, D. J. "Assessing the Impact of Employee Unionization in Community and Junior Colleges." In A. M. Hoffman and D. J. Julius (eds.), *Managing Community and Junior Colleges,* pp. 111–141. Washington, DC: College and University Personnel Association, 1994.

Kalinos, K. D. "Changes in Employment Placement." In R. I. Miller and E. W. Holzapfel, Jr. (eds.), *Issues in Personnel Management.* New Directions for Community Colleges, No. 62. San Francisco: Jossey-Bass, 1988.

Kandzer, J. W. *A Comparison of Student Ratings of Teaching Effectiveness for Full-Time Versus Part-Time Florida Community Colleges.* Unpublished doctoral dissertation, Florida State University, 1977. Dissertation Abstracts International, 38, 2509A.

Keim, M. C. "Two-Year College Faculty: A Research Update." *College Community Review*, 1989, 17 (3), 34–43.

Kempner, K. "Faculty Culture in the Community College: Facilitating or Hindering Learning." *Review of Higher Education*, 1991, 13 (2), 215–235.

Killian, Clyde B. *Professional Faculty Development Practices Used in United States Four Year Higher Education Institutions.* Unpublished doctoral dissertation, Ohio University, 1994.

King, R. W., and Cleland, D. I. *Strategic Planning and Policy.* New York: Van Nostrand Reinhold, 1978.

Kinney, D. P., and Smith, S. P. "Age and Teaching Performance." *Journal of Higher Education*, 1992, 63 (3), 282–302.

Knoell, D. M. "Serving Today's Diverse Students." In G. B. Vaughn (ed.), *Issues for Community College Leaders.* San Francisco: Jossey-Bass Publishers, 1983.

Kreider, P. E., Walleri, R. D., and Gratton, N. *Institutional Effectiveness and Student Success.* Gresham, OR: Mt. Hood Community College, 1993 (ERIC Document Reproduction Service No. ED 356–843).

Law, F.W.K. *A Comparative Analysis of Teaching Effectiveness Between Part-Time and Full-Time Faculty in Selected Ohio Two-Year Colleges.* Unpublished doctoral dissertation, Ohio University, 1987.

Lawhon, T., and Ennis, D. L. "Recruiting and Selecting Community College Faculty." *Community College Journal of Research and Practice*, 1995, 19, 349–359.

Lechtreck, R. "College Faculty Evaluation by Students—An Opportunity for Bias." *College Student Journal*, 1987, 21 (3), 297–299.

Licata, C. M., and Andrews, H. A. "Faculty Leader's Responses to Post-Tenure Evaluation Practices." *Community/Junior College Quarterly of Research and Practice*, 1990, 16 (1), 47–56.

Lincoln, Y. S. "The Structure of Promotion and Tenure Decisions in Institutions of Higher Education: A Policy Analysis." *Review of Higher Education*, 1983, 6 (3), 217–231.

Linquist, J. "Summary Recommendations." In J. Linquist (ed.), *Designing Teaching Improvement Programs*, pp. 252–277. Berkeley, CA: Pacific Soundings, 1978.

Linsky, A. S., and Straus, M. A. "Student Evaluations, Research Productivity and Eminence of College Faculty." *Journal of Higher Education*, 1975, 46, 89–102.

Lolley, J. L. "A Comparison of the Use of Instructional Resources by Full and Part-Time Teachers." *Community/Junior College Research Quarterly*, 1980, 5, 47–51.

Lowry, C. B. "The Status of Faculty Status for Academic Librarians: A Twenty-Year Perspective." *College and Research Libraries*, March 1993, 54, 163–172.

Magner, D. K. "Tenure Reexamined: Association Hopes 2-Year Study Will Lead to More Flexibility in Academic Careers." *Chronicle of Higher Education*, 1995, 41, A17–18.

Marsh, H. W., and Bailey, M. "Multidimensional Students' Evaluations of Teaching Effectiveness: A Profile Analysis." *Journal of Higher Education*, 1993, 64 (1), 1–18.

Maxwell, W. E., and Kazlaukas, J. "Which Faculty Development Methods Really Work in Community Colleges: A Review of Research." *Community/Junior College Quarterly of Research and Practice*, 1992, 16 (4), 351–360.

McCabe, R. H. "Foreword." In R. H. McCabe (ed.), *The American Community College: Nexus for Workforce Development*. Mission Viejo, CA: League for Innovation in the Community College, February 1997.

McCabe, R., and Jenrette, M. "A Place in the Sun for Teaching and Learning." *Trusteeship*, 1993, 1, 25–28.

McCadden, J. "The Adjunct Institute—A Successful Program for Adjunct Training." *Adjunct Info*, 1994, 2 (4), 1+.

McGee, R. L. "Faculty Evaluation Procedures in Eleven Western Community Colleges." *Community College Journal of Research and Practice*, 1995, 19, 341–348.

McGreal, T. L. *Successful Teacher Evaluation*. Alexandria, VA: Association for Supervision and Curriculum Development, 1983.

McKeachie, W. J., Pintrich, P. R., Lin, Y., and Smith, D.A.F. *Teaching and Learning in the College Classroom: A Review of the Research Literature*. Ann Arbor: University of Michigan, National Center for Research to Improve Postsecondary Teaching and Learning, 1986.

McManis, G.L., and Harvey, L.J. *Planning, Management, and Evaluation Systems in Higher Education*. Littleton, CO: Ireland Educational Corporation, 1978.

Menges, R. J. "Evaluation in the Service of Faculty." In P. Seldin, *Changing Practices in Faculty Evaluation: A Critical Assessment and Recommendations for Improvement*. San Francisco: Jossey-Bass, 1984.

Miami-Dade Community College. *Faculty Excellence Subcommittee Survey Report*. Miami, FL: Miami-Dade Community College, 1987.

Miami-Dade Community College. *Teaching/Learning Values at Miami-Dade Community College*. Miami, FL: Miami-Dade Community College, 1988.

Miller, D. J., and Ratcliff, J. L. "Analysis of Professional Development Activities of Iowa Community College Faculty." *Community/Junior College Quarterly*, 1986, 10 (4), 317–343.

Miller, R. I. "The Quality Movements in Higher Education in the United States." *Higher Education in Europe*, 1996, 21 (2–3), 193–202.

Miller, R. I. *Major American Higher Education Issues and Challenges in the 1990's*. London: Jessica Kingsley Publishers, 1990.

Miller, R. I. (ed.). *Evaluating Major Components of Two-Year Colleges*. Washington, DC: College and University Personnel Association, 1988.

Miller, R. I. *Evaluating Faculty for Promotion and Tenure*. San Francisco: Jossey-Bass, 1987a.

Miller, R. I. "Evaluating Teaching: The Role of Student Ratings." In R. I. Miller, *Evaluating Faculty for Promotion and Tenure*. San Francisco: Jossey-Bass, 1987b.

Miller, R. I. *The Assessment of College Performance*. San Francisco: Jossey-Bass, 1979.

Miller, R. I. *Developing Programs for Faculty Evaluation: A Sourcebook for Higher Education*. San Francisco: Jossey-Bass, 1974.

Miller, R. I. *Evaluating Faculty Performance*. San Francisco: Jossey-Bass, 1972.

Miller, R. I. *The Academic Dean*. Washington, DC: Institute for College and University Administrators, 1971.

Miller, R. I., and Holloway, M. L. "Hiring and Evaluating Community College Personnel." In A. M. Hoffman and D. J. Julius (eds.), *Managing Community and Junior Colleges*. Washington, DC: College and University Personnel Association, 1994.

Miller, R. I., and Holzapfel, E. W., Jr. (eds.). *Issues in Personnel Management*. San Francisco: Jossey-Bass, 1988.

Murray, M., and Owen, M. A. *Beyond the Myths and Magic of Mentoring*. San Francisco: Jossey-Bass Publishers, 1991.

National Commission on Higher Education Issues. *To Strengthen Quality in Higher Education*. Washington, DC: American Council on Education, 1982.

Nielson, H. D. "Assessment and Quality Assurance in Distance Teacher Education." *Distance Education*, 1997, 18 (2), 284–317.

O'Banion, T. *Teachers for Tomorrow: Staff Development in the Community-Junior College*. Tucson: The University of Arizona Press, 1973.

Opp, R. D., and Smith, A. B. "Effective Strategies for Enhancing Minority Faculty Recruitment." *Community College Journal of Research and Practice*, 1994, 18 (2), 147–163.

Parilla, R. E. "Gladly Would They Learn and Gladly Teach." Southern Association of Community and Junior Colleges Occasional Paper, 1986, 4 (1) (ERIC Document Reproduction Service No. ED 263–949).

Paris, W. "Early Academic Warning System." In B. B. Beckman (ed.), *How to Do More with Less: Community College Innovations to Increase Efficiency and Reduce Costs*. Mission Viejo, CA: League for Innovation in the Community College, 1996.

Peltason, J. W. "Foreword." In A. Tucker, *Chairing the Academic Department*. Washington, DC: American Council on Education, 1982.

Peterson, M. W., and White, T. H. "Faculty and Administrator Perceptions of Their Environments: Different Views or Different Models of Organization?" *Research in Higher Education*, April 1992, 33, 177–204.

Phillippe, K. A. *National Profile of Community Colleges: Trends and Statistics, 1997–98*. Washington, DC: Community College Press, 1997.

Piland, W. E., and Silva, C. "Multiculturalism and Diversity in the Community College Curriculum." *Community College Journal of Research and Practice*, 1996, 20, 35–48.

Ramos, S. "Faculty Advising Program." In B. Beckman (ed.), *How to Do More With Less: Community College Innovations to Increase Efficiency and Reduce Costs*. Mission Viejo, CA: League for Innovation in the Community College, 1996.

Ratcliff, J. L. "Faculty Evaluation as a Measure of Organizational Productivity." Southern Association of Community and Junior Colleges Occasional Paper No. 2, 1984 (ERIC Document Reproduction Service No. ED 235–866).

Raufman, L., Williams, D. N., and Colby, A. "The Instructional Role of Two-Year College LRC's." In N. Holleman (ed.), *The Role of the Learning Resources Center in Instruction*. New Directions for Community Colleges, 1990, 71, 103.

Reed, D., and Sork, T. J. "Ethical Considerations in Distance Education." *American Journal of Distance Education*, 1990, 4 (2), 36–42.

Rifkin, T. "ERIC Review: Faculty Evaluation in Community Colleges." *Community College Review*, 1993, 23, 63–70.

Rostek, S., and Kladivko, D. I. "Faculty Development Models." In R. I. Miller and E. W. Holzapfel, Jr. (eds.), *Issues in Personnel Management*. New Directions for Community Colleges, No. 62. San Francisco: Jossey-Bass, 1988.

Roueche, J. E., Roueche, S. D., and Milliron, M. D. "Identifying the Strangers: Exploring Part-Time Faculty Integration in American Community Colleges." *Community College Review*, 1996, 23, 33–48.

Saaty, T. L., and Ramanujam, V. "An Objective Approach to Faculty Promotion and Tenure by the Analytic Hierarchy Process." *Research in Higher Education*, 1983, 18, 311–331.

Sands, R. G., and others. "Faculty Mentoring in a Public University." *Journal of Higher Education*, 1991, 62 (2), 98–107.

Scott, O. P. *A Study to Design and Recommend a Faculty Development Model for Promoting Professional Growth and Instructional Change*. Unpublished doctoral dissertation, Pepperdine University, 1987. Dissertation Abstracts International, 48, 2229A.

Scriven, M. "Value vs. Merit." *Education*, 1978, 8, 1.

Seldin, P. *Changing Practices in Faculty Evaluation: A Critical Assessment and Recommendations for Improvement*. San Francisco: Jossey-Bass, 1984.

Seldin, P. *Successful Faculty Evaluation Programs: A Guide to Improve Faculty Performance and Promotion/Tenure Decisions*. Crugers, NY: Coventry, 1980.

Shawl, W. F. *Professional Development Programs That Work*. Paper presented at the 64th Annual Convention of the American Association of Community and Junior Colleges, Washington, DC, 1984 (ERIC Document Reproduction Service No. ED 243–513).

Shonebarger, J. E. "Point Twelve: Remove Barriers That Rob People of Pride of Workmanship." In R. I. Miller (ed.), *Applying the Deming Method to Higher Education*. Washington, DC: College and University Personnel Association, 1991.

Smith, A. B. "Innovations in Staff Development." In T. O'Banion (ed.), *Innovation in the Community College*, pp. 177–199. New York: Macmillan, 1989.

Smith, A. B. (ed.). *Evaluating Faculty and Staff*. New Directions for Community Colleges, No. 41. San Francisco: Jossey-Bass, 1983.

Smith, A. B. *Staff Development Practices in U.S. Community Colleges*. Lexington, KY: AACJC National Council for Staff, Program, and Organizational Development, 1980.

Smith, A. B. *Faculty Development and Evaluation in Higher Education*. ERIC/Higher Education Research Paper, No. 8. Washington, DC: The American Association for Higher Education, 1976.

Smith, A. B., and Barber, J. A. "Faculty Evaluation and Performance Appraisal." In A. M. Cohen and F. B. Brawer (eds.), *Managing Community Colleges: A Handbook for Effective Practice*, pp. 382–438. San Francisco: Jossey-Bass, 1994.

St. Clair, K. L. "Faculty-to-Faculty Mentoring in the Community College: An Instructional Component of Faculty Development." *Community College Review*, 1994, 22, 23–26.

Susman, M. B. "Where in the World Is the Colorado Electronic Community College?" *Community College Journal*, 1997, 68 (2), 16–20.

Taylor, F. W. *The Principles of Scientific Management*. New York: Harper and Row, 1911.

Traylor, C. F. *A Comparative Analysis of Selected Criteria Used in Four-Year Colleges and Universities to Evaluate Teaching, Scholarship, and Service and Faculty Overall Performance*. Unpublished doctoral dissertation, Ohio University, 1992.

Twigg, C. A., and Oblinger, D. G. "The Virtual University." Report presented at the Joint Educom/IBM Roundtable, Washington, DC, 1997.

U.S. Department of Education. *The Chronicle of Higher Education, Facts and Figures*. Washington, D.C., August 28, 1993, p. 5.

Vaughn, G. B. *The Community College Story: A Tale of American Innovation*. Washington, DC: American Association of Community Colleges, 1995.

Vaughn, G. B. "Scholarship and the Community College Professional: Mandate for the Future." Paper presented at the 69th Annual Convention of the American Association of Community and Junior Colleges, Washington, DC, 1989 (ERIC Document Reproduction Service No. ED 305–965).

Vaughan, G. B., and Weisman, I. M. "Selected Characteristics of Community College Trustees and Presidents." *New Directions for Community Colleges*, Summer 1997, 25 (2), 5–12.

Walker, B. D. "An Investigation of Selected Variables Relative to the Manner in Which a Population of Junior College Students Evaluate Their Teachers." *Dissertation Abstracts*, 1969, 29 (9-B), 3474.

Weimer, M. *Improving College Teaching*. San Francisco: Jossey-Bass, 1990.

Wilson, L. *The Academic Man*. New York: Oxford University Press, 1942.

Wyler, Jean C. "How We Work: A Corporate View of Campus Practices." *AAHE Bulletin*, 1992, 44 (8), 4–8.

Zitlow, E. *Faculty Evaluation Procedures Used in Two-Year Postsecondary Educational Institutions*. Unpublished doctoral dissertation, Ohio University, 1988.

Index

Academe, 119
Accountability, 6–7, 118
Adjunct Faculty Institute, 35–36
Alberta, Canada, 13
Aleamoni, L. M., 48–49
Alfred, R. L., 20, 24–25
American Association of Community and Junior Colleges (AACJC), 23–24
American Council on Education, 46
Americans with Disabilities Act (ADA), 97
Andrews, H. A., 10–11, 114
Annual Developmental Review (ADR), 15, 97–98, 107, 123
Annual Performance Review (APR), 15, 97, 107–10, 123, 163–70
Arreola, R. A., 16, 17–18
Astin, A. W., 18, 135
Avakian, A. N., 95

Bacon, Francis, 92
Bailey, M., 47
Barnsley, J. R., 27
Battle Creek, Michigan, 34

Bellevue Community College (BCC). *See* Developing a faculty evaluation system
Boyer, C. M., 59
Boyer, Ernest, 30
Braskamp, L. A., 49, 50, 101
Brawer, F. B., 5
Building Communities: A Vision for a New Century: A Report of the Commission on the Future of the Community College, 23–24
Burlington County Community College, 35

California, 67
Carter, D. J., 96
Centra, John, 135; professional development and, 76, 77, 78, 124; student evaluation of faculty and, 48, 49, 50, 54; Zitlow study and, 27, 46
Chair evaluation, 7, 28, 54–57, 58
Chief executive officers (CEOs), 5
Classroom teaching, 3, 47–54
Classroom visitation, 28–30, 55–57, 72, 74, 137–38

Coffeyville Community College,
  39
Cohen, A. M., 5, 18
Colby, A., 22
Colleague evaluation, 7
College advisory committees
  (CACs), 5
College Policies and Procedures Manual, 31
College service, 58–59
Colorado Electronic Community
  College, 117–18
Columbus State Community College, 21
Commission on the Future of
  Community Colleges, 30
Community College Consortium,
  19–20
Community College Effectiveness
  Study, 19–20
Community colleges. *See* Two-
  year colleges; *specific subject
  matter*
Community service, 58–59
Costin, L., 47–48
Creech, F. R., 50

Dean evaluations, 28, 59–60
Deming, W. Edwards, 6, 116
Determining Faculty Effectiveness,
  27
Developing a faculty evaluation
  system, 63; areas of evaluation
  and, 148; assumptions statement and, 147; commitment to,
  158; development link and, 157–
  58; establishing committee for,
  143–45; feedback on plan for,
  153–55; final document
  distribution and, 155–57; grievance procedure and, 153; instrument of evaluation and, 149–51;
  objectives of system and, 148;
  preparing committee for, 146–47;

process/procedure development and, 151–52; purposes of
  evaluation and, 147; review of
  system and, 157; standards/
  weights and, 153; student evaluations and, 64–65; training im-
  plementers and, 158
Disabled, 97
Distance learning, 116–21
"Distance Learning: A Report,"
  119

Educational Resources Informa-
  tion Center (ERIC), 22
Educational Testing Services
  (ETS), 40, 46, 72
Education Index, 6–7
Efficiency, 7
Evaluation. *See* Faculty evaluation
  (systems)

Faculty and Staff Development
  Fund, 67
Faculty evaluation (systems), 66;
  accountability and, 6–7; administrator evaluation and, 126; annual written reports and, 15;
  apprehension over, 7; chair
  evaluation and, 54–57; change
  opposition and, 17–18; classroom performance and, 14;
  classroom teaching and, 47–54;
  classroom visitation and, 28–30,
  55–57, 137–38; college advisory
  committees and, 5; college service and, 58–59; data sources
  and, 3; dean evaluation and, 28,
  59–60; diversity and, 2; evaluation of, 9–10; evaluators' qualifications and, 16–17; faculty job
  satisfaction and, 24; faculty
  scholarship and, 30–32; fairness
  of, 27; growth of, 33–34; history
  of, ancient, 126; importance of,

13; improvement/development of, 45; institutional climate and, 15–16, 20–22; institutional-individual needs balance and, 15; institutional values and, 12–13, 25; manageability of, 26–27; objectives for, 45, 46; organizational/operational links and, 14; part-time faculty and, 36–37; performance improvement and, 12; personal attributes and, 60; planning-doing-evaluating circle and, 8–9, 15, 115–16; post-tenure evaluations and, 10–11; proactive climate for, 12–18; professional development programs and, 78–79; professional preparation and, 60; purpose of, 26, 32, 126–27; recommended improvements for, 129–30; regularity of, 14; reviewing evaluation criteria and, 10–11; reviewing problem outcomes and, 11; senior administrative staff and, 16; of senior instructors, 14; student advising and, 60, 62–63; teaching load and, 3; teaching materials and, 141–42; total quality management movement and, 8–10; Zitlow study on, 3, 27–28, 46–47, 48. *See also* Developing a faculty evaluation system; Future of evaluation; Student evaluation of faculty; Tenure/promotion process
Faculty Excellence Subcommittee, 159
Faculty exchange programs, 75
Faculty service, 58
Fillmore, Millard, 123
Finley, C. E., 24
Future of evaluation, 124; annual reviews and, 123; creative improvements and, 123–24; creativity/imagination and, 116; distance learning and, 116–21; faculty improvement programs and, 115, 116, 124; government support and, 113–14; institutional goals and, 115; management role and, 116; need for system and, 121–22; organizational-operational links and, 122–23; performance improvement and, 122; planning ahead and, 121; post-tenure review and, 114–15; responsibility for evaluation and, 115–16

Gage, N. L., 50
Gappa, J. M., 41
Gleason, M., 49
Graber, J. S., 36–37
Greece, 126
Grievance procedure, 105, 153
Grymes, R. J., 40–41
Gustad, J. W., 135

Hammons, J. O., 27
Harper, William Rainey, 1
Hefferlin, J. B., 100
Heisenberg, W., 66
Highet, Gilbert, 22
Hiring faculty, 93–97
Hocking Technical College, 34–35
Hopple, T. G. (faculty development study by), 72; administration and, 82; evaluation of programs and, 78–79; faculty involvement and, 76; funding and, 7–8, 77–78, 124; organizational structures and, 76–78; student advising and, 60, 62; student evaluations and, 72, 74–75
Houston Community College, 1–2, 39

"Identifying the Strangers: Exploring Part Time Faculty Integration in American Community Colleges," 41
Individualized instructional load (IIL), 107–10
Internet, 117–18

Jenrette, M., 99
Joliet Junior College, 1

Kansas, 39
Kellogg Community College, 34
Kempner, K., 19
Ken, Clark, 98–99
Kladivko, D. I., 87

Law, F.W.K., 40, 41
Learning resource centers (LRCs), 22
Lee, C.B.T., 135
Leslie, D. W., 41
Lethbridge Community College (LCC), 13, 25
Lewis, D. R., 59
Librarians, 22–23
Licata, C. M., 10–11, 114
Lincoln, Y. S., 123
Linder, V. P., 20
Linquist, J., 70
Lolley, J. L., 40–41
Lowery, C. B., 22–23

Magner, D. K., 96–97
Marsh, H. W., 47
Maryland, 31
McCabe, R., 99
McCadden, J., 35–36
McGee, R. L., 97
McGreal, T. L., 55–56
McKeachie, W. J., 47–48
Menges, R. J., 116
Mentoring, 37–39

Miami-Dade Community College, 1, 13, 25, 85, 131–33
Michigan, 34
Miller, R. I., 48, 49, 87, 106
Milliron, M. D., 41
Modified Student Instructional Report (MSIR), 40
Monroe County Community College, 34
Montgomery County, Maryland, Community College, 31
Murray, M., 37

National Commission on Higher Education Issues, 114
National Institute for Staff and Organizational Development (NISOD), 82
Nelsonville, Ohio, 34–35
Nielson, H. D., 118–19

Ohio, 21, 40
On Innovation, 92
Ory, J. C., 49, 50, 101
Owen, M. A., 37

Parilla, R. E., 31
Paris, W., 39
Part-time faculty, 33, 34–37, 40–43, 95–96
Peltason, J. W., 54
Pemberton, New Jersey, 35
Peterson, M. W., 20, 24–25
Piland, W. E., 96
Planning-doing-evaluating circle, 8–9, 15, 115–16
Principles of learning, 159–61
Professional development/improvement (programs): accountability and, 6–7; Annual Developmental Review and, 97–98; annual evaluations and, 83; basic assumptions of, 83; basic components of, 85–86; cost of,

70, 71; diversity and, 2, 67; evaluation objectives and, 46; evaluation of, 78–79, 82–86; faculty exchange programs and, 75; faculty involvement in, 76; faculty visitations and, 75; failure-prone strategies and, 92; funding for, 7–8, 77–78, 124; future and, 115, 116, 124; implementation of, 90–92; institutional values and, 71; investment in, 67; leadership of, 81–82; matrix model for, 87–90; models of, current, 82; need for, 7, 67–69, 79–80; operational principles of, 83, 85; organizational structures for, 76–78; purposes of, 70; quality of, 70–71; resistance to, 69–70; specialists and, 74–75; staff support toward, 71; student evaluations and, 72, 74–75; total quality management movement and, 8–10. *See also* Tenure/promotion process

Quality Instruction Program (QIP), 35

Ramos, S., 39
Ratcliff, J. L., 26
Raufman, L., 22
Reed, D., 118
Rostek, S., 87
Roueche, J. E., 41
Roueche, S. D., 41

St. Clair, K. L., 38–39
Scholarship Reconsidered, 30
Scriven, M., 101
Seldin, P., 28–29, 135
Self-evaluation, 7, 28, 58, 139–40
Silva, C., 96
Smith, A. B., 77

Sork, T. J., 118
Southern Regional Education Board Survey, 26
"Statement of Faculty Excellence," 25
Student advising, 39–40, 60, 62–63
Student evaluation of faculty: accountability and, 7; age of teachers and, 49–50; classroom teaching and, 3, 47–54; class size and, 48; developing instruments for, 51; distributing/gathering rating forms and, 51, 53–54; gender and, 49; grades received and, 48–49; part-time faculty and, 36, 40; professional development and, 72, 74–75; reliability/validity of, 47–50; student advising and, 63; teacher personality and, 49; Zitlow study and, 28
Student evaluation of teaching effectiveness (SETE) forms, 47
Student population, 1–2, 33

Tappan, Henry, 1
Taylor, F. W., 7
Teaching improvement process (TIP) model, 82
"Teaching/Learning Values," 13, 131–33
"Teaching Tips," 34
Technical colleges. *See* Two-year colleges
Tenure/promotion process, 99–100; Annual Performance Review and, 107–10; consistency of, 103–4; credibility of, 106–7; fairness of, 103–4, 106; grievance procedure and, 105; institutional/departmental expectations and, 102; institutional goals/objectives and, 100–101; institutional history/nature

and, 100; institutional-
individual needs balance and,
101–2; legality issues and, 106;
manageability of, 104–5; purposes of, 98–99; written policy
statements on, 103
Three Thousand Futures, 99
Total quality management (TQM),
6, 8–10
Traylor, C. F., 29, 135
Two-year colleges: as client-
oriented, 6; community needs
and, 3–5; conception of, 1; cur-
ricular/instructional flexibility
and, 5–6; diversity in, 2, 96; effectiveness study on, 24–25; faculty importance in, 111; faculty
morale and, 24; governance
processes in, 5; growth of, 33;
hiring faculty and, 93–97; identifying faculty and, 22–23; institutional culture and, 19–22; as
integral part of higher educa-

tion, 1–2, 18; intellectual environment of, 23; measuring
quality of, 126; mentoring and,
37–39; minority faculty and, 96–
97; student population of, 1–2;
teaching load and, 23. *See also
specific subject matter*

"Uncertainty principle," 66
University of Central Florida, 120
University of Chicago, 1

Vaughan, G. B., 2, 31, 96

Walker, B. D., 50
Washington, 63
Weisman, I. M., 96
White, T. H., 20, 24–25
Williams, D. N., 22
Wilson, Logan, 12

Zitlow, E., 3, 10–11, 27–28, 30, 46–
47, 48, 58, 78–79

About the Authors

RICHARD I. MILLER is Professor of Higher Education at Ohio University. He is the author of several texts on higher education.

CHARLES FINLEY is Professor of Graphic Communications at Columbus State Community College.

CANDACE SHEDD VANCKO is President, State University of New York, College of Technology Delhi.